Brick Math Series

# TEACHING SUBTRACTION USING LEGO® BRICKS

Dr. Shirley Disseler

*Teaching Subtraction Using LEGO® Bricks*

Copyright ©2017 by Shirley Disseler
Published by Brigantine Media/Compass Publishing
211 North Avenue, St. Johnsbury, Vermont 05819

Cover and book design by Anne LoCascio
Illustrations by Curt Spannraft
All rights reserved.

Your individual purchase of this book entitles you to reproduce these pages as needed for your own classroom use only. Otherwise, no part of this book may be reproduced or utilized in any way or by any means, electronic or mechanical, including photocopying, recording, or information storage or retrieval system, without prior written permission from the publisher. Individual copies may not be distributed in any other form.

Brigantine Media/Compass Publishing
211 North Avenue
St. Johnsbury, Vermont 05819
Phone: 802-751-8802
Fax: 802-751-8804
E-mail: neil@brigantinemedia.com
Website: www.compasspublishing.org
www.brickmath.com

LEGO®, the LEGO® logo, and the Brick and Knob configurations are trademarks of the LEGO® Group, which does not sponsor, authorize, or endorse this book. All information and visual representations in this publication have been collected and interpreted by its author and do not represent the opinion of the LEGO® Group.

ORDERING INFORMATION
**Quantity sales**
Special discounts for schools are available for quantity purchases of physical books and digital downloads. For information, contact Brigantine Media at the address shown above or visit www.brickmath.com.

**Individual sales**
Brigantine Media/Compass Publishing publications are available through most booksellers. They can also be ordered directly from the publisher.
Phone: 802-751-8802 | Fax: 802-751-8804
www.compasspublishing.org
www.brickmath.com
ISBN 978-1-9384066-7-6

# CONTENTS

Introduction.................................5

**Chapter 1:** What Does It Mean to Subtract?..........11

**Chapter 2:** Ten-Frames Subtraction Within 20........16

**Chapter 3:** Missing Term Subtraction ...............23

**Chapter 4:** Decomposing Numbers / Place Value .....31

**Chapter 5:** Result Unknown Problems Within 20 .....39

**Chapter 6:** Change Unknown Problems Within 20 ....51

**Chapter 7:** Start Unknown Problems Within 20.......64

**Appendix**..................................74
  • Suggested Brick Inventory
  • Student Assessment Chart
  • Baseplate Paper

## DEDICATION

In memory of my mother, who gave me passion for teaching children, and in honor of my dad, who continually inspires me to create!

# INTRODUCTION

Subtraction is one of the first computational skills that children learn in school. But children really begin to subtract as preschoolers when they begin to separate things or give items to others. If you ask a young child to give you two blocks and keep three blocks, the idea of taking away from the total is being imprinted.

Students must learn the *why* and *how* behind the process of subtraction. Teachers often turn subtraction into addition to get the result, which does not help the student understand the concept of subtraction. The process of repeated subtraction leads to the understanding of division, so if a student has a firm understanding of subtraction concepts, he or she is more likely to be successful with division.

Vocabulary is very important when learning how to subtract. Words such as *minuend, subtrahend, difference, result, solution, minus*, and *take away* are content words that young learners must grasp. The symbol of subtraction, the minus sign, should be thoroughly explained when discussing what is happening in a problem. Teachers of mathematics should use the action of the math so that children can attach words to their understanding of the subtraction process.

The strategies garnered from mastery of early skills such as *counting on, counting back, one more than*, and *one less than* provide a strong foundation for understanding subtraction (Cathcart, Pothier, Vance, and Bezuk, 2015). Researchers have identified three distinct types of subtraction problems children need to learn to solve: *start unknown, change unknown*, and *result unknown*. Comparison also plays a huge

Cathcart, W. George, Yvonne M. Pothier, James H. Vance, and Nadine S. Bezuk, *Learning Mathematics in Elementary and Middle Schools: A Learner-Centered Approach*. Boston: Pearson Education, 2014.

role in subtraction problems because it matches the way the brain works when solving word problems. The use of direct modeling is beneficial to young learners because it provides a visual representation that leads to the understanding behind the action of the math (Cathcart et al.). Attaching concrete objects to the action of symbols in math leads to deeper conceptual thinking when problem solving.

Why use LEGO® bricks to learn about subtraction?

LEGO® bricks help students learn mathematical concepts through modeling. If a student can model a math problem and then be able to understand and explain the model, he or she will begin the computational process without struggling. Using LEGO® bricks to model subtraction helps show the action of subtraction so students can visualize what is happening in a problem. Modeling with LEGO® bricks is an easy way for students to demonstrate their understanding of the vocabulary and the concept of subtraction.

LEGO® bricks are great tools for bringing many mathematical concepts to life: basic cardinality and counting, addition and subtraction, multiplication and division, fractions, data and measurement, and statistics and probability. Using LEGO® bricks fosters discussion, modeling, collaboration, and problem solving. These are the $21^{st}$-century skills that will help students learn and be globally competitive.

The use of a common child's toy to do math provides a universal language for math. Children everywhere recognize this manipulative. It's fun to learn when you're using LEGO® bricks!

# HOW TO TEACH WITH THE BRICK MATH SERIES

**Using the *Teaching* and *Learning* Books:**
Start by taking students through the **Part 1: Show Them How** section of each chapter. Build the models, show them to the students, and ask students questions. Where directed, have students build the same models themselves so they are manipulating the bricks as you are guiding them. A document camera is helpful to display your models to the whole class as you build them. The step-by-step directions in the *Teaching* books work through several problems in Part 1. If you are using the companion *Learning* books, which are the Student Editions, have students draw their models and answer the questions in those books as you teach using the *Teaching* book.

Once students have mastered the modeling processes from Part 1, move to the **Part 2: Show What You Know** section of the chapter. Ask students to complete each of the problems using bricks and drawing their models. The companion *Learning* books (Student Editions) have space for writing answers and baseplate paper for drawing models. Move through the room and check that students are building their models correctly, drawing them clearly, and understanding the concepts being taught.

The *Learning* books (Student Editions) include an assessment for each chapter, as well as additional problems for practice and challenge. The books also include an Assessment Chart

to track each student's performance on all the skills taught in the *Addition* book.

*Note:* Active learning breeds active learners! Students will be motivated and engaged in math when they are using bricks. It will not be silent in your classroom, but it will be full of chatter about the math!

**Suggested Bricks:**
The Brick Math Series is designed to be used with basic LEGO® bricks. If you already have LEGO® bricks in your classroom, your students should be able to use them to make the models. They may have to combine smaller bricks together when the directions call for longer bricks such as 1x10s or 2x12s. Each student also needs a baseplate on which to build brick models.

Each chapter lists the bricks suggested for the lessons in that chapter for every two students, and the book includes a total brick inventory that lists all the bricks suggested for the program for every two students.

Specially designed Brick Math brick sets for one or two students are available for purchase from Brigantine Media. Brick sets are packaged in divided boxes and include a baseplate for each student.

**Classroom Management Ideas:**
- Before starting, have a conversation with the students about using bricks as a learning tool rather than a toy.
- Teach students the language of bricks (baseplate, stud, 1x1, 1x2, etc.).
- Assign brick sets to specific students and always give the same students the same sets. An easy way to do this is to number each brick set and assign the sets to pairs of students by number. When students know that they will always have to work with the same brick set, they are more likely to be careful that the bricks are returned to the set.
- Do not teach using bricks—or any manipulative—every day. Students also need to have opportunities to think through the math processes without having a physical object for modeling. Sometimes it helps to have students draw models without building them with bricks

first. Remember, they won't have access to manipulatives during most tests when they have to show what they have learned.
- To keep bricks clean: Put the bricks in a hosiery bag and wash them on the top rack of the dishwasher. Let them air dry. Clean bricks before assigning sets to new students.
- To keep bricks from sliding off desks, use foam shelf liner cut into rectangular pieces, or large meat trays (you can often get these free from a local supermarket).
- Inventory the sets twice a year and replace bricks as needed. There are a variety of vendors online that sell specific bricks, both new and used. LEGO® retail stores also sell a variety of individual bricks.

# WHAT DOES IT MEAN TO SUBTRACT?

**Students will learn/discover:**
- How to subtract within 20
- The definition of *subtraction*
- What is means to subtract two numbers
- How to write mathematical equations for subtraction models

**Why is this important?**
Understanding the vocabulary of subtraction is important to put math number/word relationships together. Young learners must be able to demonstrate how subtraction works and what it means to have some "left over." One-to-one correspondence, visualization, and modeling are strategies student will continue to use as they mature in math understanding.

**Vocabulary:**
- Subtract: Move from the whole
- Minuend: Largest number (and usually the first number) in a subtraction problem; the number that the subtrahend is subtracting from
- Subtrahend: Smaller of two numbers (and usually the second number) in a subtraction problem; the number that is being subtracted from the minuend
- Minus: Symbol in a subtraction problem

### SUGGESTED BRICKS

| Size | Number |
|------|--------|
| 1x1  | 10     |
| 1x2  | 10     |
| 1x3  | 8      |
| 1x4  | 8      |
| 1x6  | 4      |
| 1x10 | 2      |
| 2x2  | 4      |
| 2x3  | 6      |
| 2x4  | 4      |

Note: Using a baseplate will help keep the bricks in a uniform line. One baseplate is suggested for these activities.

**How to use the companion student book, *Learning Subtraction Using LEGO® Bricks*:**
- After students build their models, have them draw the models and explain their thinking in the student book. Recording the models on paper after building them with bricks helps reinforce the concepts being taught.
- Discuss the vocabulary for each lesson with students as they work through the student book.
- Use the assessment in the student book to gauge student understanding of the content.

## Part 1: Show Them How

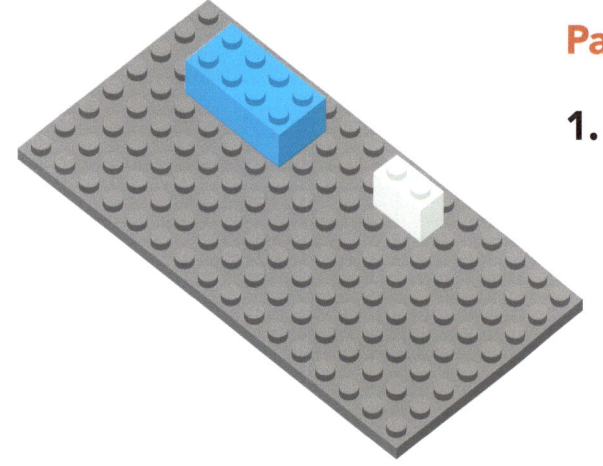

1. Build a model of the number 8 using one 2x4 brick. Have students make the same model. Build a model of the number 2 by placing two 1x1 bricks or one 1x2 brick to the right of the 2x4 brick, leaving space between the two models. Explain to students that these models represent the two parts of a subtraction problem: The 2x4 brick represents the *minuend* of 8 and the 1x2 brick represents the *subtrahend* of 2. Have students draw the two models and label the parts of the problem.

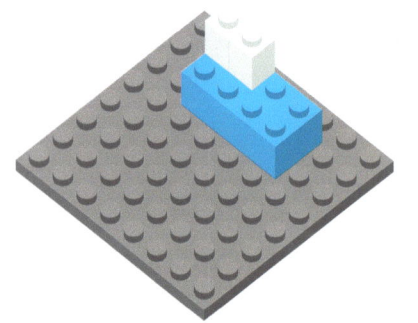

2. Show the subtraction of 8 studs – 2 studs by placing the 1x2 brick on top of the 2x4 brick. Ask students how many studs are not covered (6).

   Explain that the uncovered studs are called the *difference*, which is how many are left after subtracting. Have students show this step on their models.

   Have students draw the solution and label the numbers represented by the bricks.

   Show students how to write a mathematical statement for the model: 8 studs – 2 studs = 6 studs.

**3.** Build a model of the number 10 using a 1x10 brick. Have students build the same model and draw it.

Explain to students that this model represents the start of the subtraction problem. Ask students to give the name for that number (*minuend*).

**4.** Build a model of the number 3 to the right of the model for the number 10. Ask students to give the name for that number (*subtrahend*). Have students add a model for 3 to their models and draw it.

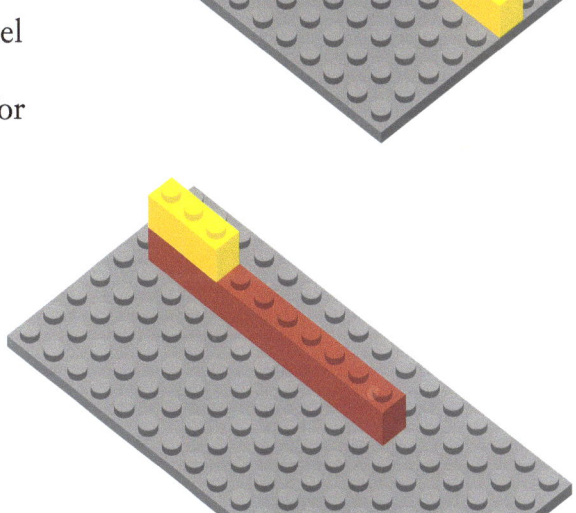

**5.** Have students model the *difference*. Ask students how they know how much the *difference* is in this problem. Have students write an explanation of their thinking.

**6.** Have students write a mathematical sentence for this problem.

Have students draw the model that shows the *difference* and label it.

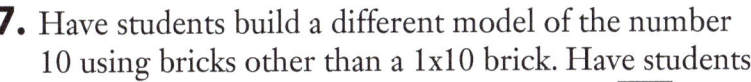

**7.** Have students build a different model of the number 10 using bricks other than a 1x10 brick. Have students build a model to show: 10 studs – 6 studs = ☐ studs

*Possible solution:*

Have students share their models with a partner. Each student should draw his/her model and explain each part of his/her problem.

Five 1x2 bricks represent the minuend of 10. One 2x3 brick represents the subtrahend of 6. Six studs on top of 10 studs leaves 4 studs showing. The 2x2 brick proves that 4 are left.

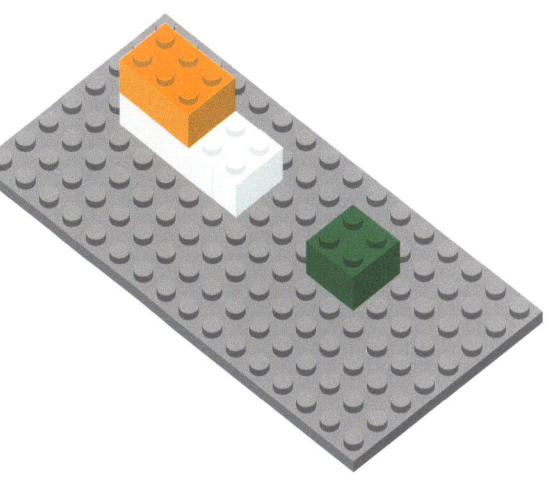

## Part 2: Show What You Know

**1.** Can you build a model that shows the number 6 and a model that shows the number 2? Can you build a model that shows the difference between 6 and 2? Draw your model. Label the drawing with subtraction vocabulary words. Write a math sentence for the problem.

*Possible solution:*

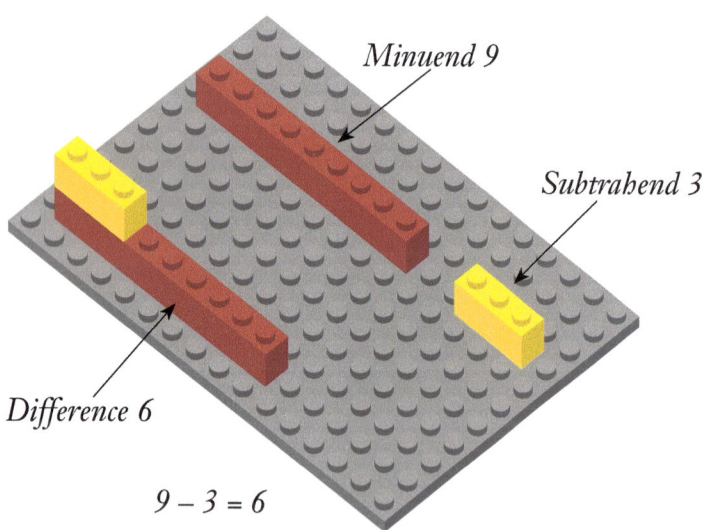

Minuend 6
Subtrahend 2
Difference 4

6 – 2 = 4

**2.** Can you build a model that shows the number 9 and a model that shows the number 3? Can you build a model that shows the difference between 9 and 3? Draw your model. Label the parts of the drawing with subtraction vocabulary words. Write a math sentence for the problem.

*Possible solution:*

Minuend 9
Subtrahend 3
Difference 6

9 – 3 = 6

**3.** Can you build a model for this mathematical sentence?
5 studs – 2 studs = 3 studs

Draw and explain your model in writing. Label all the parts of the model (*minuend*, *subtrahend*, *difference*).

5 studs represent the minuend and 2 studs represent the subtrahend. Placing the subtrahend on top of the minuend shows the difference of 3 studs.

*Possible solution:*

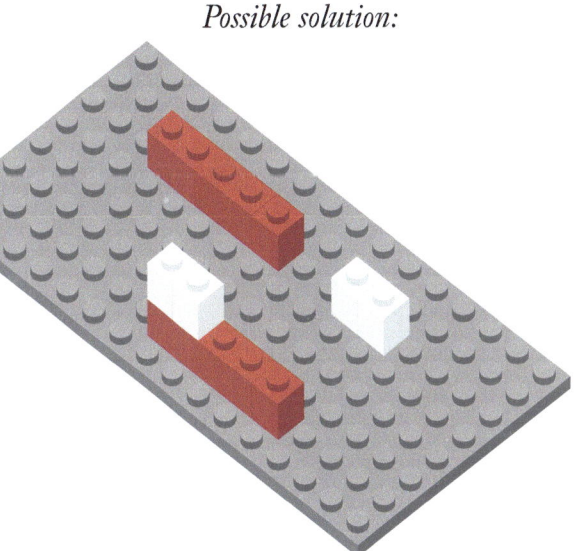

**4.** Can you build a model that shows each part of this math sentence? 8 studs – 4 studs = ☐ studs

Draw and explain your model in writing. Label all the parts of the model (*minuend*, *subtrahend*, *difference*).

*Possible solution:*

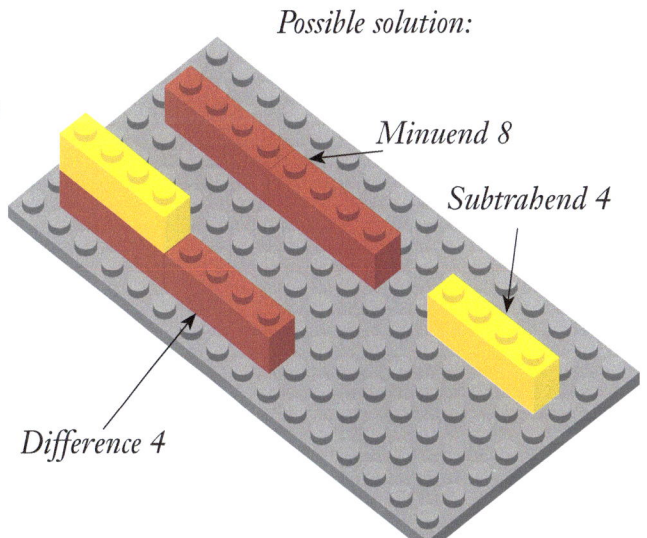

Minuend 8
Subtrahend 4
Difference 4

## Challenge:

Model a subtraction problem with bricks. Do not include the difference in the model. Find a partner and exchange problems. Solve your partner's problem. After you have both completed the problems, discuss your solutions and make sure you can explain both models. Draw both models and your solutions. Write your explanations of both models.

## SUGGESTED BRICKS

| Size | Number |
|------|--------|
| 1x1  | 20     |
| 1x2  | 10     |
| 1x3  | 4      |
| 2x3  | 6      |
| 2x4  | 8      |

Note: Using a baseplate will help keep the bricks in a uniform line. One baseplate is suggested for these activities.

# TEN-FRAMES SUBTRACTION WITHIN 20

**Students will learn/discover:**
- How to subtract within 20

**Why is this important?**
Modeling the subtraction of numbers within twenty allows students to combine early number skills such as one-to-one correspondence with the understanding of *less than* and *more than*. This fosters the ability to perform mental math with regard to sets of ten as they grow more proficient. Repeated subtraction helps students find solutions in division. The ability to conceptually understand subtraction leads to greater success when they get to higher levels of math.

**Vocabulary:**
- Ten-Frame: bricks in 2x5 configuration to show a set of 10
- Subtract: Move from the whole
- Minuend: Largest number (and usually the first number) in a subtraction problem; the number that the subtrahend is subtracting from
- Subtrahend: Smaller of two numbers (and usually the second number) in a subtraction problem; the number that is being subtracted from the minuend
- Difference: Solution to a subtraction problem
- Minus: Symbol in a subtraction problem

**How to use the companion student book, *Learning Subtraction Using LEGO® Bricks*:**
- After students build their models, have them draw the models and explain their thinking in the student book. Recording the models on paper after building them with bricks helps reinforce the concepts being taught.
- Discuss the vocabulary for each lesson with students as they work through the student book.
- Use the assessment in the student book to gauge student understanding of the content.

**Review of ten-frames (From *Teaching Counting and Cardinality Using LEGO® Bricks*):**
If students have not used ten-frames, teach this strategy first, and then move to the addition activities with ten-frames. *Note:* You may need to review working with ten-frames even if students learned it earlier.

**1.** Build two *ten-frames* on a baseplate. Show your models to the students and have them each build two ten-frames. *Note:* A ten-frame has a 2x5-stud configuration, but there are no 2x5 LEGO® bricks. To build a ten-frame, use one 2x4 brick and one 1x2 brick of the same color or one 2x2 brick and one 2x3 brick of the same color.

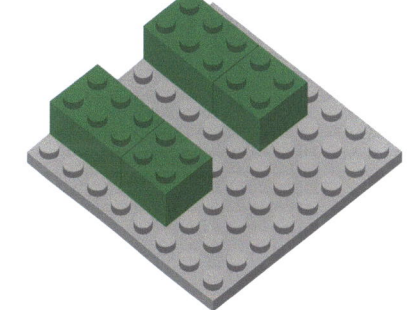

Ask students to count the number of studs in each ten-frame. Students should count 10. Discuss with them that this model is called a *ten-frame* and is used to model numbers in sets of ten.

**2.** Ask students to place one 1x1 brick on top of each stud in the first ten-frame.

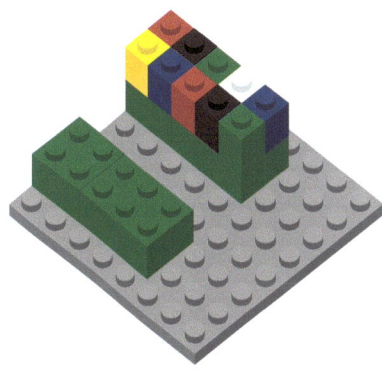

Students should be able to use one-to-one correspondence to count to ten. Have students draw their models.

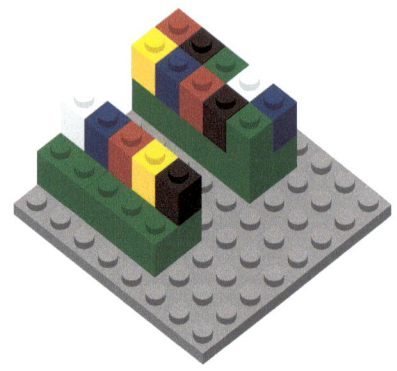

**3.** Now work with the second ten-frame. Ask students to place enough 1x1 bricks to fill the top row of the second ten-frame. Have students write the number of studs used and draw their models. Students should count 5 studs.

Ask students to look at both ten-frames. Have students count to determine which ten-frame models the larger number and explain why. Have students record their results in writing. Students should say that the top ten-frame models the larger number because it shows 10 studs, while the bottom one shows 5 studs.

## Part 1: Show Them How

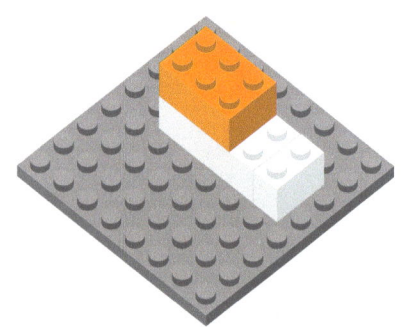

**1.** Ask students to count to 6 and show you six fingers. Build a ten-frame using bricks of one color. Build a model of the number 6 on the ten-frame using one 2x3 brick. Show students your model and have them build the same model. Have students count the number of studs in the model along with you. Have students draw the model.

**2.** Build a model of the number 4 on the same baseplate with one 2x2 brick. *Note*: It is best to select a different color brick for this number.

Explain to students that the 2x2 brick represents the *subtrahend* of 4, which is the number being subtracted from 6. Have students build the same model and draw it.

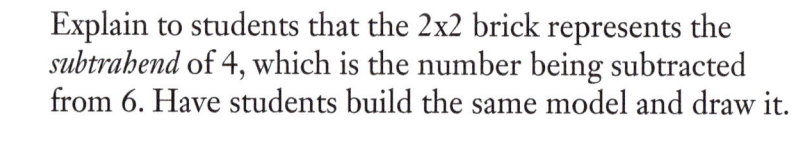

**18** TEACHING SUBTRACTION USING LEGO® BRICKS | DR. SHIRLEY DISSELER

3. Have students model the subtraction by placing the 2x2 brick on top of the 2x3 brick. Have students draw the models.

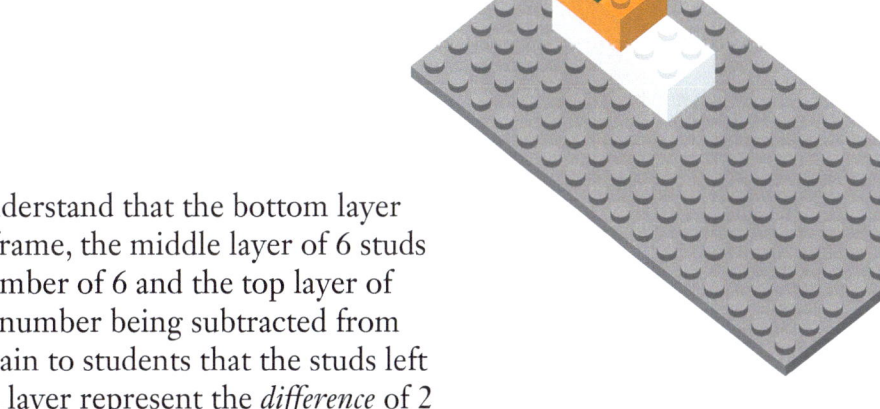

4. Make sure students understand that the bottom layer of 10 studs is the ten-frame, the middle layer of 6 studs represents the start number of 6 and the top layer of 4 studs represents the number being subtracted from the start number. Explain to students that the studs left showing in the middle layer represent the *difference* of 2 studs.

   Show students how to write the math sentence for this problem: 6 – 4 = 2

5. Build a model of the number 12 using two ten-frames. Have students build the same model.

6. Choose a brick to represent the number 8 (a 2x4 brick works well). Place this brick on the baseplate. Have students build the model and draw it. Have students write a math sentence for this problem.

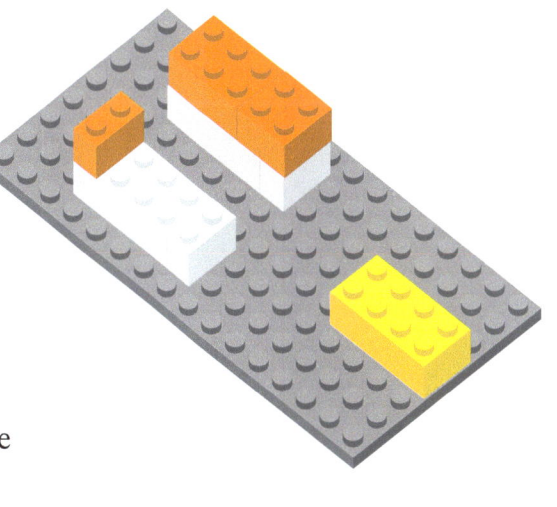

7. Combine the models to show subtraction by placing the 8 studs on the 12 studs. Count with students to demonstrate that the model shows 4 studs left uncovered, which is the *difference* of 4. Have students draw the models.

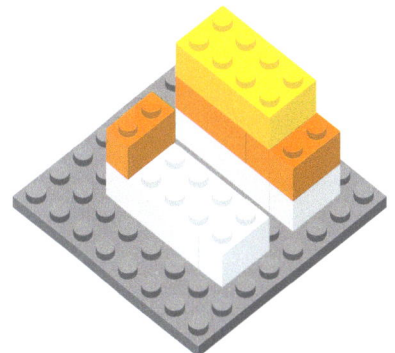

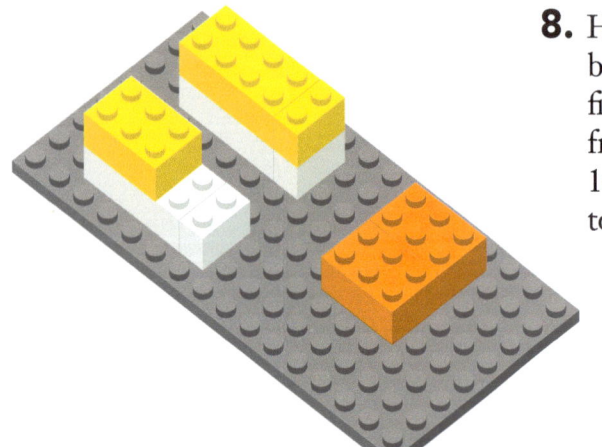

**8.** Have students build a model to show the difference between 16 and 12. They should build two ten-frames first. Then students should place bricks on the ten-frames that have 16 studs in total to show the *minuend* of 16. Next, students should place bricks with 12 studs in total on the baseplate to show the *subtrahend* of 12.

Students should combine the two models by placing the 12 studs on top of the 16 studs.

*Possible solutions:*

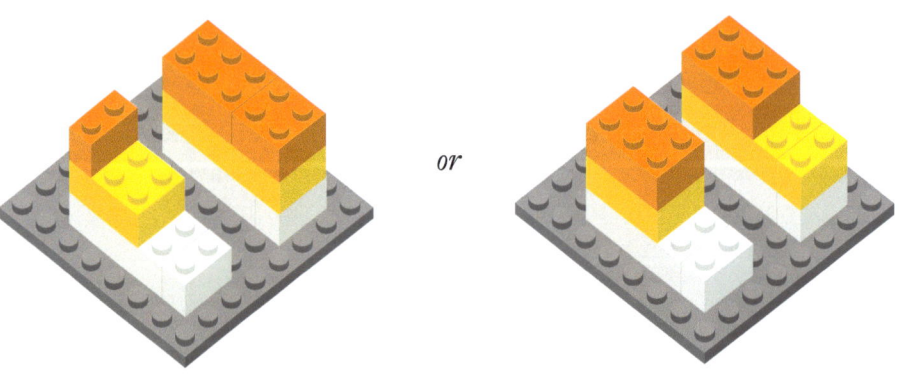

Look top down to see how many of the 16 studs are not covered. Point out that this solution is the *difference* of 4.

Have students draw the models.

**20** TEACHING SUBTRACTION USING LEGO® BRICKS | DR. SHIRLEY DISSELER

## Part 2: Show What You Know

**1.** Can you model the subtraction of 12 – 8? Build two ten-frames and show both sets of numbers. Build another model to show how you found the solution. Draw your models and label all the parts. Write a math sentence for your model.

*Possible solutions:*

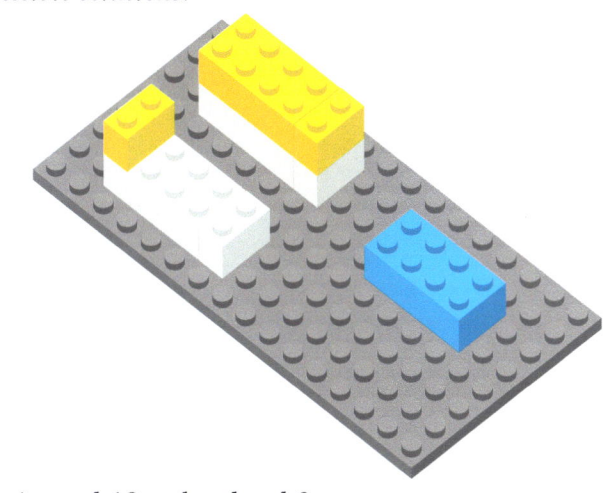

minuend 12, subtrahend 8

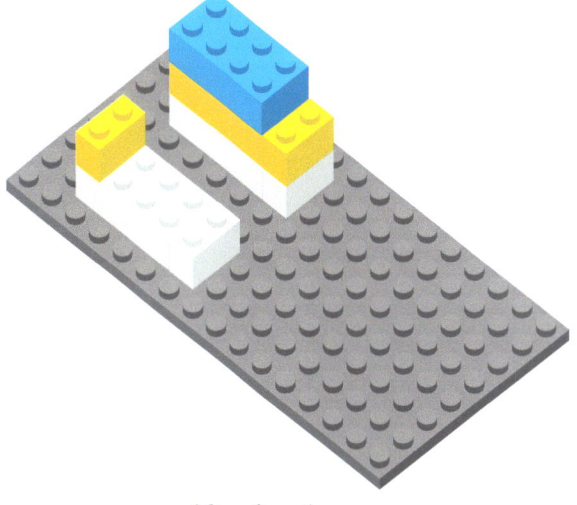

12 – 8 = 4

**2.** Can you build a ten-frame model of 14 – 5? Show both sets of numbers. Build another model to show how you found the solution. Draw your models and label all the parts. Write a math sentence for your model.

*Possible solution:*

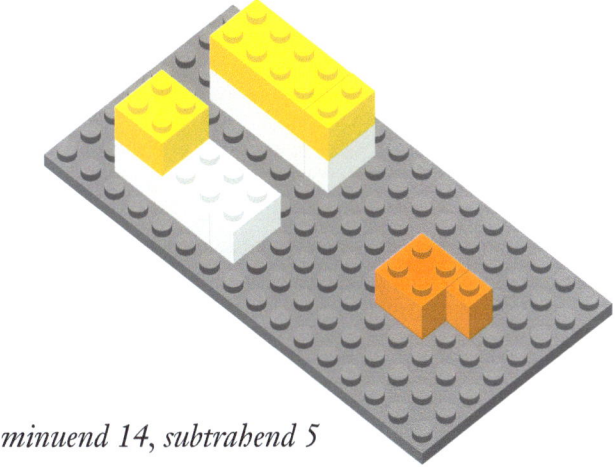

minuend 14, subtrahend 5

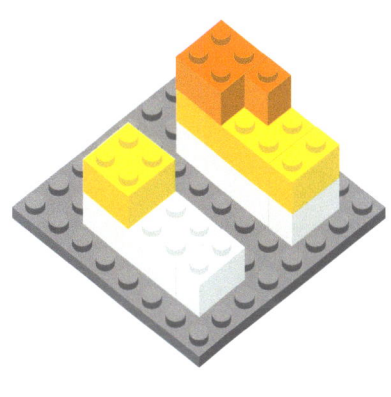

14 – 5 = 9

**3.** Can you build a ten frame model of 20 – 8? Show both sets of numbers. Build another model to show how you found the solution. Draw your models and label all the parts. Write a math sentence for your model.

*Possible solutions:*

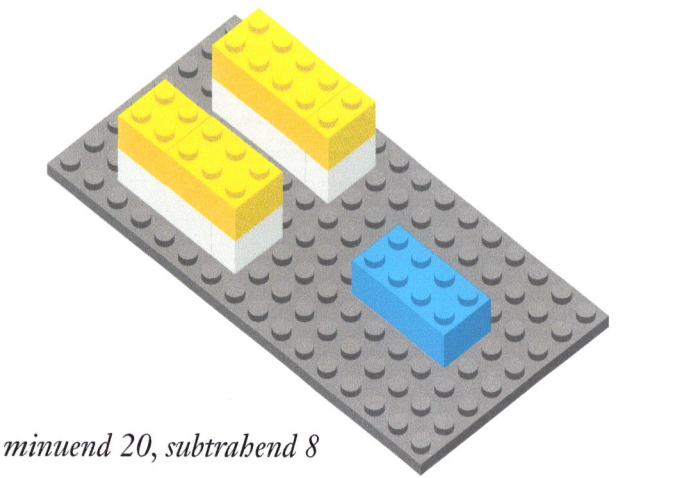

minuend 20, subtrahend 8

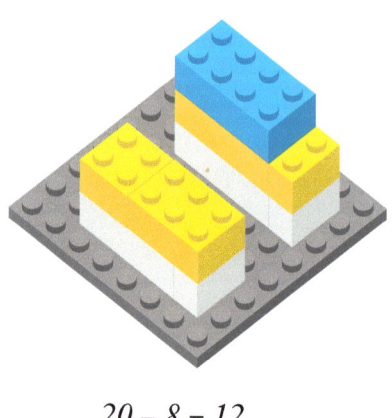

20 – 8 = 12

**4.** Can you build a ten-frame model of 6 – 6? Show both sets of numbers. Build another model to show how you found the solution. Draw your models and label all the parts. Write a math sentence for your model.

*Possible solutions:*

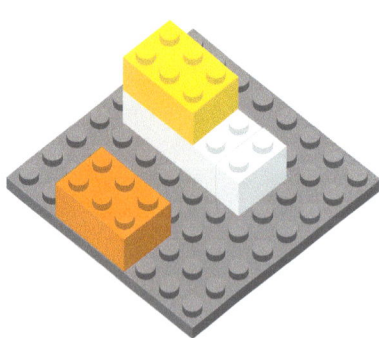

minuend 6, subtrahend 6

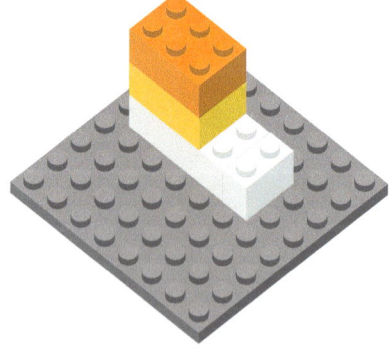

6 – 6 = 0

# MISSING TERM SUBTRACTION

**Students will learn/discover:**
How to subtract numbers within 20
How to find the missing term in subtraction problems

**Why is this important?**
Students need to understand the relationship between numerical operations. The ability to utilize addition strategies to find solutions to subtraction problems, and vice versa, leads to the development of invented strategies, which help students later with mental math and fact recall.

**Vocabulary:**
- Subtract: Move from the whole
- Minus: Symbol in a subtraction problem
- Decompose: Break apart a number to regroup
- Minuend: Largest number (and usually the first number) in a subtraction problem; the number that the subtrahend is subtracting from
- Subtrahend: Smaller of two numbers (and usually the second number) in a subtraction problem; the number that is being subtracted from the minuend
- Difference: solution to a subtraction problem

## SUGGESTED BRICKS

| Size | Number |
|---|---|
| 1x1 | 10 each of 4 colors |
| 1x2 | 4 |
| 1x3 | 4 |
| 1x8 | 4 |
| 1x10 | 2 |
| 1x12 | 2 |
| 2x2 | 6 |
| 2x3 | 4 |
| 2x4 | 4 |
| 2x6 | 4 |
| 2x8 | 2 |
| 2x10 | 2 |

Note: Using a baseplate will help keep the bricks in a uniform line. One baseplate is suggested for these activities.

**How to use the companion student book, *Learning Subtraction Using LEGO® Bricks*:**

- After students build their models, have them draw the models and explain their thinking in the student book. Recording the models on paper after building them with bricks helps reinforce the concepts being taught.
- Discuss the vocabulary for each lesson with students as they work through the student book.
- Use the assessment in the student book to gauge student understanding of the content.

## Part 1: Show Them How

1. Draw the subtraction diagram and have students draw it. (If you are using the *Learning Subtraction Student Edition* books, the subtraction diagrams for the problems are in the book.) Explain to students that the box labeled with the letter M represents the first number in the problem, or the *minuend*. The box labeled with the letter S represents the second number in the problem, or the *subtrahend*. The box labeled with the letter D represents the *difference*. Explain that in these problems a different term is missing (*start number, change number,* or the *result number*). Start to discuss with students invented strategies that they might use to find the missing term in the problem. As you discuss strategies with students, note if the chosen strategies are reasonable and can be built and drawn.

|   | M |
|---|---|
| − | S |
|   | D |

**2.** Show students a 2x6 brick and a 2x2 brick and have students find those bricks. Ask students to count the number of studs on each brick, draw the bricks, and record that number of studs for each brick.

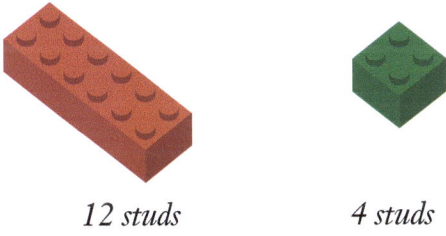

*12 studs*     *4 studs*

**3.** Have students put the 2x6 brick on the M box. Have students put the 2x2 brick on the S box.

Ask students how to find the number that goes in the box labeled D. Have students discuss strategies to find the solution with a partner. Have students model their ideas and create a math sentence that describes the model.

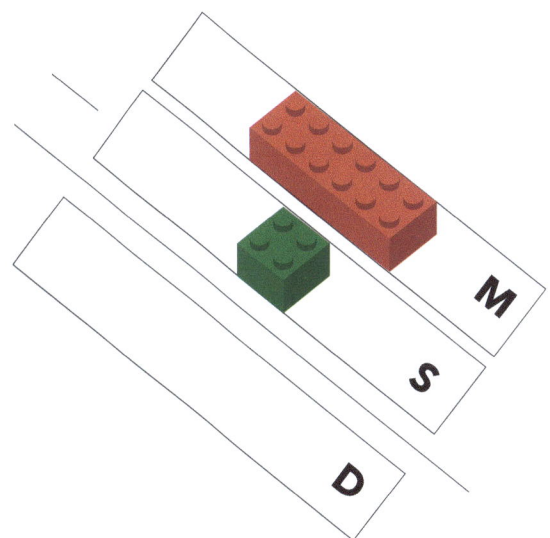

One strategy students might discover is to place a 2x2 brick on top of a 2x6 brick and count the studs that are not covered.

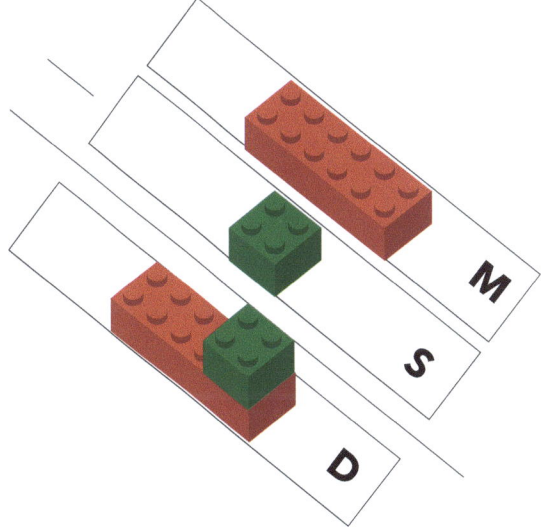

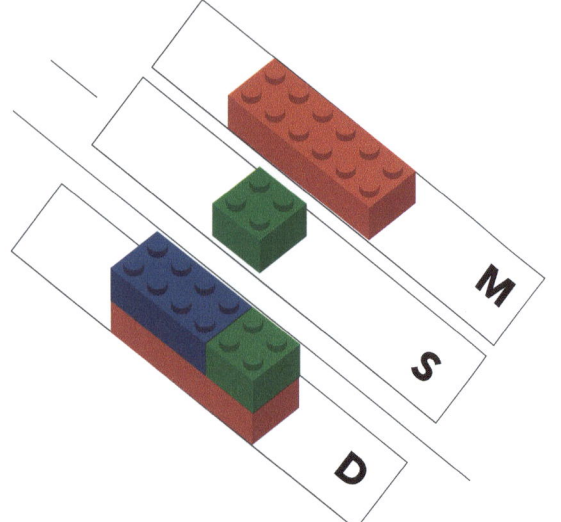

Another strategy students might discover is to find parts of the whole and match up the amounts. They may model the 8 studs left over after taking away 4 studs from 12 studs, using a 2x4 brick. *Note:* It is not acceptable for a student to simply place an 8-stud brick in the D box since that does not show the process.

Have students choose a strategy for solving the problem and model it. Have students draw the whole problem and label each part of the problem.

**4.** Have students draw a subtraction diagram and label the boxes M, S, and D. Ask students to find one 2x4 brick and one 1x2 brick. Have students count the total studs on each brick, then draw the bricks and label them.

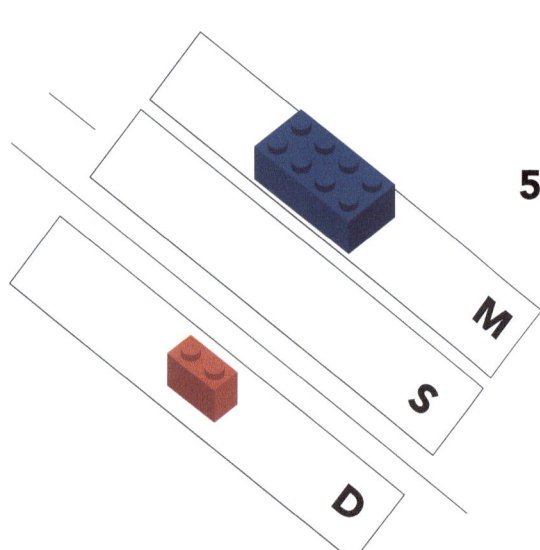

**5.** Have students place the brick with the larger number of studs (the 2x4 brick) in the M box. Have students place the brick with the smaller number of studs (the 1x2 brick) in the D box.

**6.** Ask students what the S box means. Answers can include: the amount missing, the change amount, the subtrahend, or the amount that the first number is reduced by or changed by. Ask students what goes in the S box. Have them discuss with a partner and make models of their strategies.

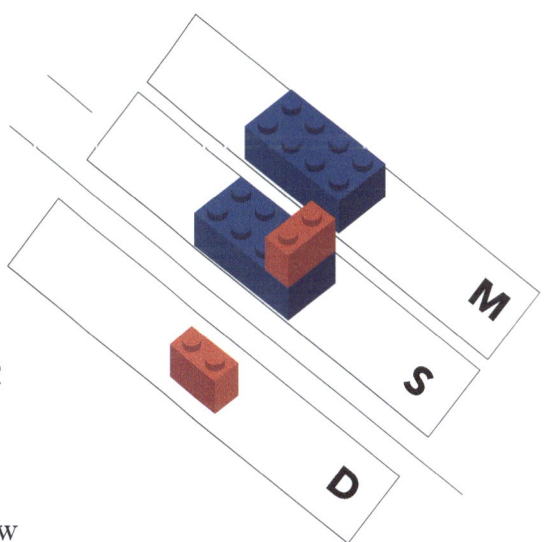

One strategy is to place a 1x2 brick on top of a 2x4 brick, then count the studs that are not covered. (6 studs uncovered) Students should understand that the 2 studs placed on top of the 8 studs represent the difference in the problem, not the amount taken away. *Note:* This shows true subtraction. Students should be aware that this is the same strategy as was used before, but now is in a different location.

Another strategy students might discover is part-part-whole, placing the 1x2 brick on top of the 2x4 brick, then filling in the uncovered studs with a 2x3 brick. Students should be able to see the relationship here between 6 + 2 = 8 and 8 – 6 = 2. Students who use this model should be able to articulate this relationship.

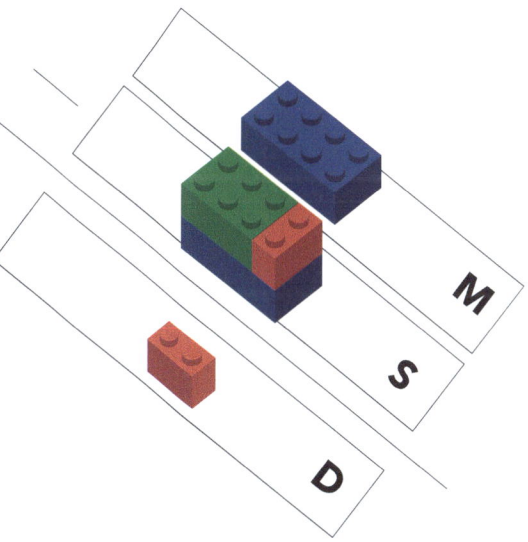

Have students place the bricks corresponding to the parts of the math sentence in the correct boxes on their diagrams. Have students draw and label the parts of the problem and write the math sentence. (8 – 6 = 2)

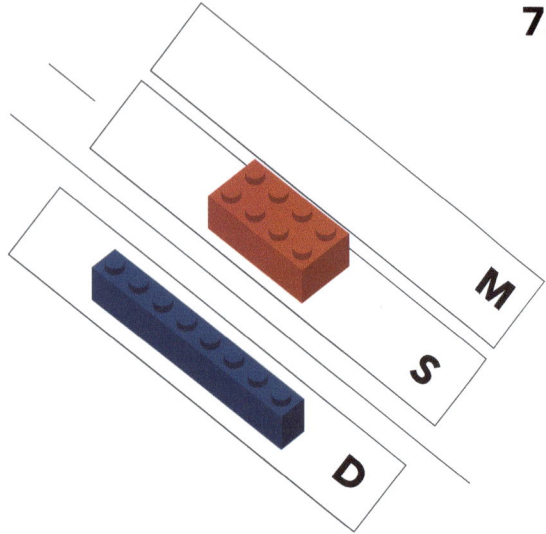

**7.** Challenge students to see different models of the same numerical value: Have students find one 2x4 brick and one 1x8 brick. Discuss how these bricks are alike and different. Students should recognize that they both have 8 studs, but one has 2 rows of 4 studs and one has 1 row of 8 studs; also, one is thinner than the other.

Have students draw a subtraction diagram and label the boxes M, S, and D. Have students place the 2x4 brick in box S and place the 1x8 brick in box D.

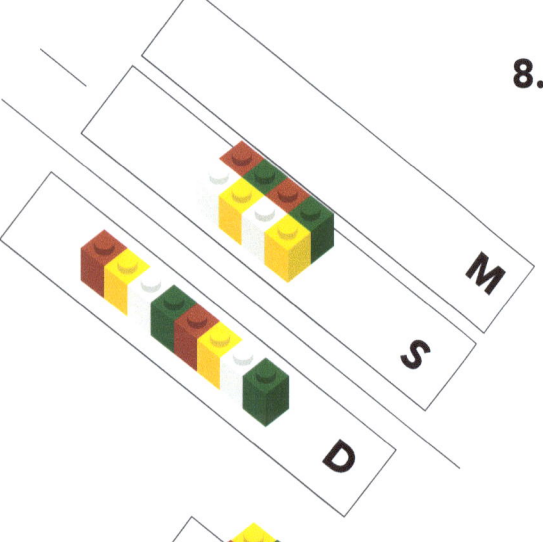

**8.** Ask students what brick goes in box M. Have students work with a partner to discuss possible solutions.

Students might use a strategy of substituting the 2x4 brick and 1x8 brick for 1x1 bricks. Using one-to-one correspondence, they would count the studs and find 16 total studs.

They would then find another brick with 16 total studs (a 2x8 brick) and place it in the M box. *Note:* While this is the correct solution, it does not show the "why." To show the process, students need to place the eight 1x1 bricks from box S on top of the 2x8 brick in box M to prove that the missing studs in the whole is equivalent to the number of studs in box S.

Students might also place all the studs on the 2x8 brick to prove that the parts of the whole are 8 and 8.

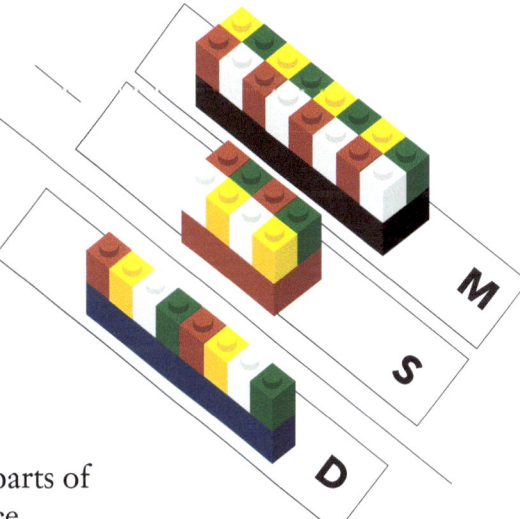

**9.** Have students draw their solution and label the parts of the problem. Have students write a math sentence.
(16 studs – 8 studs = 8 studs)

## Part 2: Show What You Know

**1.** Model the problem: 6 – 2 = ☐   Use this process:
  • Choose one brick to show 6 and another brick to show 2.
  • Draw both bricks and label the number of studs on each brick.
  • Draw a subtraction diagram of M – S = D.
  • Place the 6-stud brick in box M.
  • Place the 2-stud brick in box S.
  • Find the number that goes in box D and model the solution.
  • Draw your model on the subtraction diagram and label all the parts of the problem.
  • Write a math sentence for your model.

**2.** Model the problem: 20 − ☐ = 8
- Choose one brick to show 20 (or more bricks that total 20 studs) and another brick to show 8.
- Draw the bricks and label the number of studs on each brick.
- Draw a subtraction diagram of M − S = D.
- Place the 20-stud brick or bricks in box M.
- Place the 8-stud brick in box D.
- Find the number that goes in box S and model the solution.
- Draw your model on the subtraction diagram and label all the parts of the problem.
- Write a math sentence for your model.

**3.** Model the problem ☐ − 8 = 2
- Choose one brick to show 8 and another brick to show 2.
- Draw the bricks and label the number of studs on each brick.
- Draw a subtraction diagram of M − S = D.
- Place the 8-stud brick in box S.
- Place the 2-stud brick in box D.
- Find the number that goes in box M and model the solution.
- Draw your model on the subtraction diagram and label all the parts of the problem.
- Write a math sentence for your model.

## Challenge:

Model the problem: 20 − 4 − 6 = ☐
- Choose one or more bricks to show 20, another brick to show 4, and another brick to show 6.
- Draw the bricks and label the number of studs on each brick.
- Draw a subtraction diagram of M − S − S = D.
- Place the 20-stud brick (or bricks) in box M.
- Place the 4-stud brick in one box S.
- Place the 6-stud brick in the other box S.
- Find the number that goes in box D and model the solution.
- Draw your model on the subtraction diagram and label all the parts of the problem.
- Write a math sentence for your model.

# DECOMPOSING NUMBERS / PLACE VALUE

**SUGGESTED BRICKS**

| Size | Number |
|---|---|
| 1x1 | 10 each of 4 colors |
| 1x2 | 4 |
| 1x3 | 4 |
| 1x6 | 2 |
| 1x8 | 2 |
| 1x10 | 6 |

Note: Using a baseplate will help keep the bricks in a uniform line. One baseplate is suggested for these activities.

Note: Other bricks could be used instead of 1x1 bricks if students can visualize appropriately. For example, a 1x6 brick could represent the number 6 rather than six 1x1 bricks. But at this stage, students often need to use one-to-one correspondence when decomposing.

### Students will learn/discover:
How to subtract using decomposing

### Why is this important?
Using decomposing strategies to subtract helps students make a connection to the role of base ten in the number system.

### Vocabulary:
- Decompose: Break apart a number to regroup
- Minuend: Largest number (and usually the first number) in a subtraction problem; the number that the subtrahend is subtracting from
- Subtrahend: Smaller of two numbers (and usually the second number) in a subtraction problem; the number that is being subtracted from the minuend
- Difference: solution to a subtraction problem

**How to use the companion student book, Learning Subtraction Using LEGO® Bricks:**
- After students build their models, have them draw the models and explain their thinking in the student book. Recording the models on paper after building them with bricks helps reinforce the concepts being taught.
- Discuss the vocabulary for each lesson with students as they work through the student book.
- Use the assessment in the student book to gauge student understanding of the content.

## Part 1: Show Them How

**1.** Build a model for the problem:

22 studs − 8 studs = ☐ studs

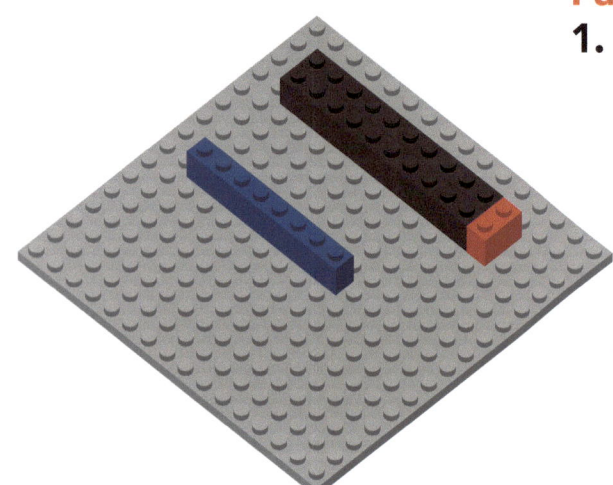

Use two 1x10 bricks and one 1x2 brick to show the minuend of 22. Use one 1x8 brick to show the subtrahend of 8. Show the model to students and discuss the use of place value and decomposing to determine the solution to the subtraction problem.

**2.** Show how to model the process of decomposing: Pull the bricks representing 22 apart. Take one 1x10 brick and add the two 1x1 bricks next to it to show 12 in the ones place.

Show the number 22 in this way:

| Tens | Ones |
|---|---|
| 1 | 12 |

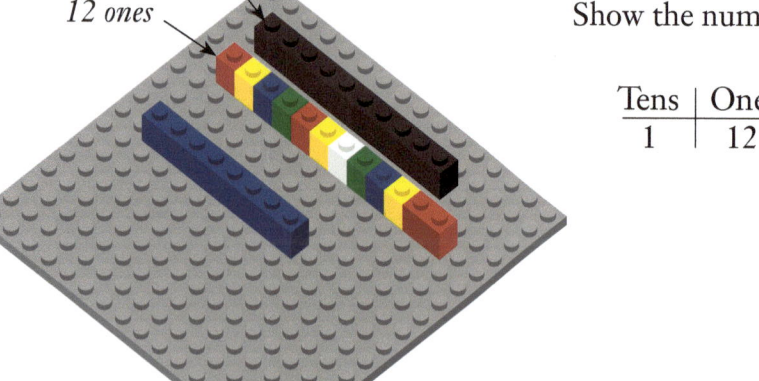

**3.** Place the 1x8 brick (subtrahend) on top of the 12 ones. Four uncovered bricks are shown.

Explain that this shows 4 ones left from the 12 ones after taking away 8 ones.

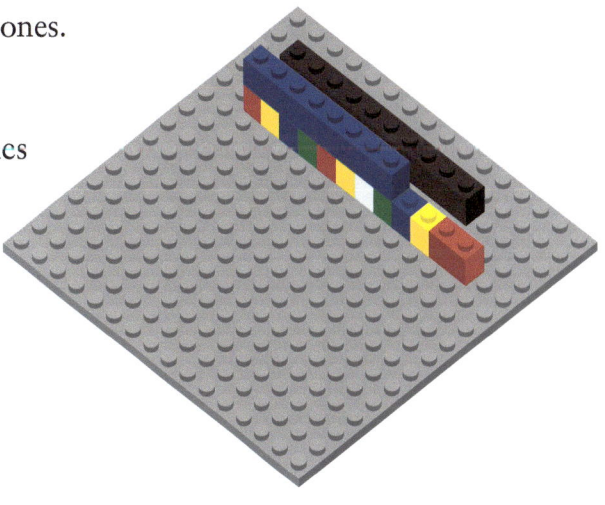

**4.** Use four 1x1 bricks to represent the 4 left. Then bring down the other 1x10 brick and put it next to the four 1x1 bricks. Count with the students to show that there are 14 studs left altogether when the numbers are composed.

The solution shows 1 ten and 4 ones, or 10 + 4 = 14.

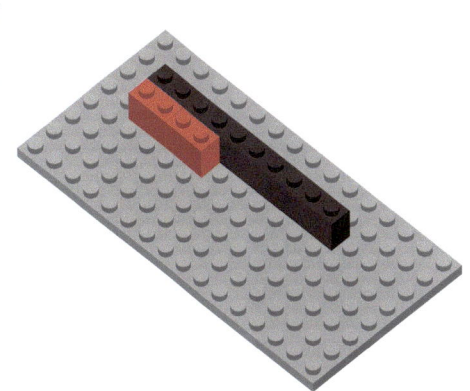

**5.** Have students check by reversing the operation:
14 + 8 = 22

Have students draw their models and label the parts of the problem.

**6.** Build a model for the problem:

33 studs – 16 studs = ☐ studs

Use three 1x10 bricks and one 1x3 brick to show the minuend of 33. Use one 1x10 brick and one 1x6 brick to show the subtrahend of 16. Have students build the model along with you.

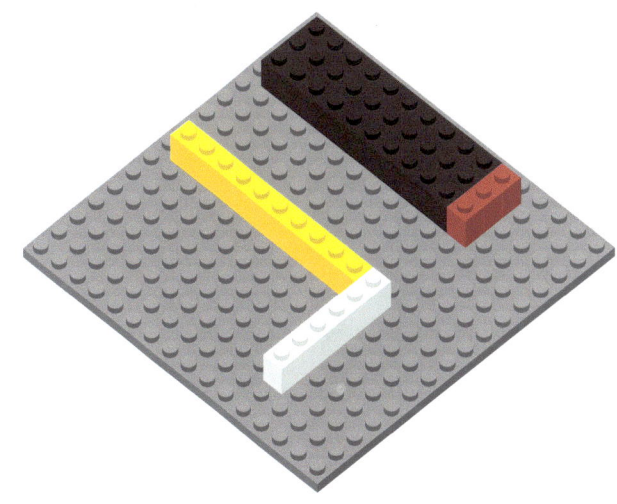

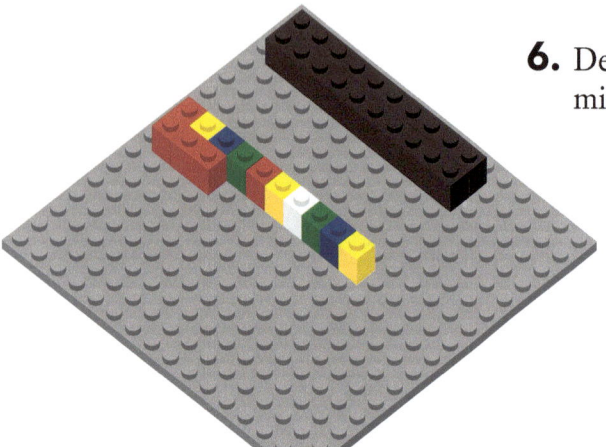

**6.** Decompose one 1x10 brick and the 1x3 brick from the minuend bricks into 13 ones, using 13 1x1 bricks.

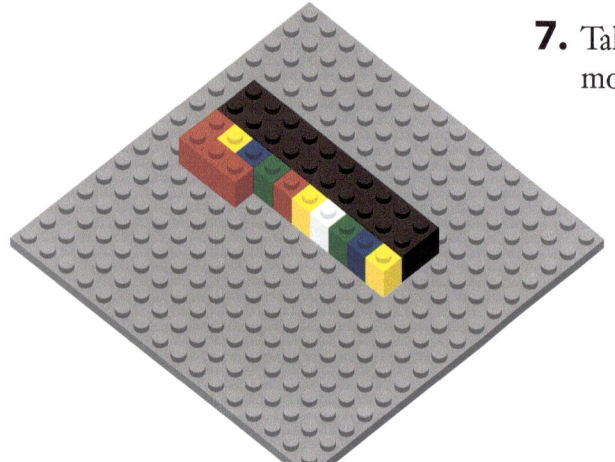

**7.** Take the remaining two 1x10 bricks from the minuend model and place them next to the 13 1x1 bricks.

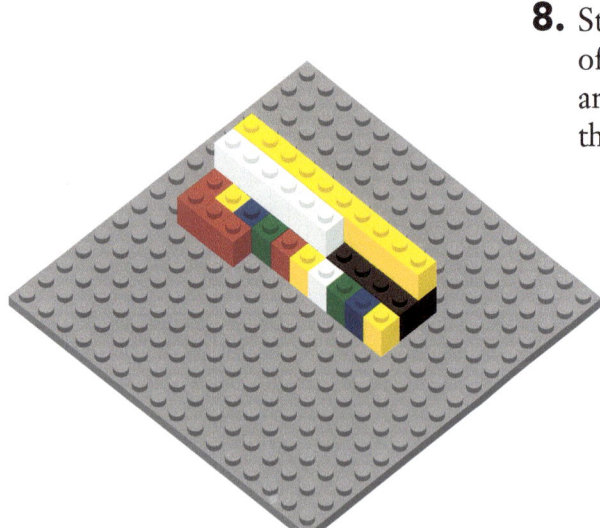

**8.** Stack the 1 ten and 6 ones from the subtrahend on top of the minuend bricks. One ten is covered and 6 ones are covered, leaving 17 studs uncovered. The solution to the problem (the *difference*) is 17 studs.

## Part 2: Show What You Know

**1.** Can you build a model to show this math sentence?

26 studs – 19 studs = ☐ studs

Show all the steps, including the decomposing of the tens into ones. How many studs are showing in your solution?

Draw the model of your solution. Explain how you found your solution.

*Possible solution:*

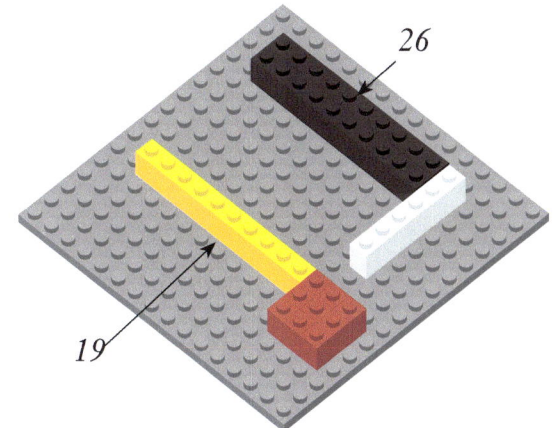

minuend 26, subtrahend 19

decomposing 1 ten and 6 ones from the minuend

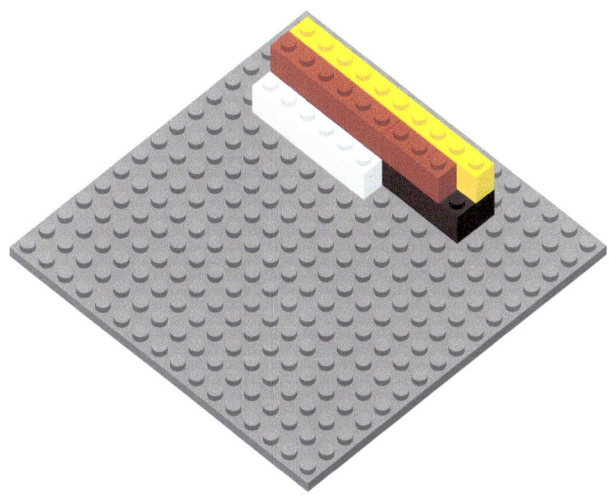

solution: 7 studs showing

*Possible solution:*

**2.** Can you work with a partner to build a model to show this math sentence? 32 studs – 16 studs = ☐ studs

Show all the steps including the decomposing of the tens into ones.

How many studs are showing in your solution? _____

Draw the model of your solution. Explain how you found your solution.

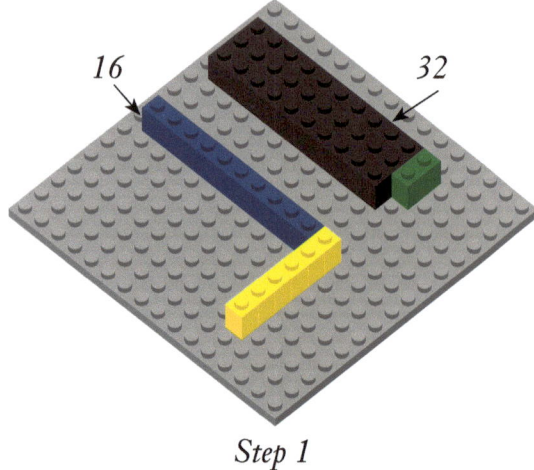

Step 1

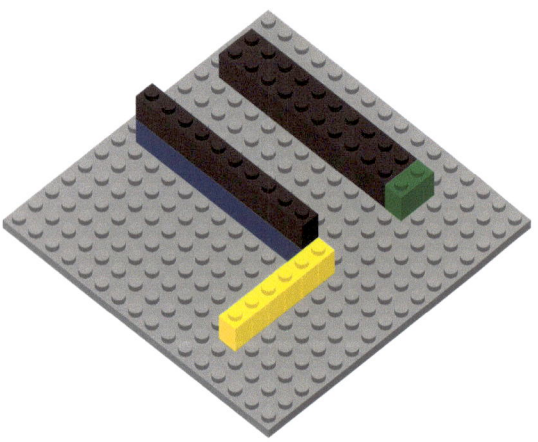

Step 2: Place one ten from minuend on top of ten from subtrahend. Remove both to show when subtracted, they are equivalent to zero.

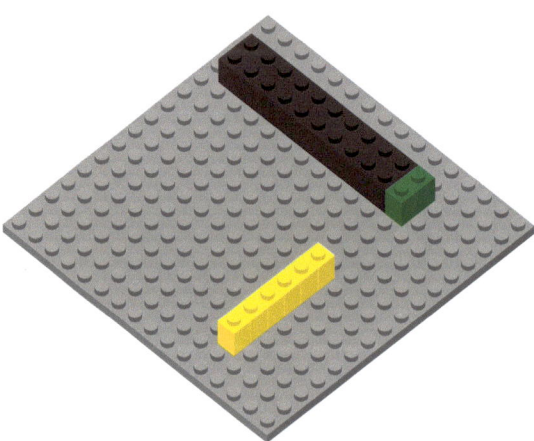

Step 3: Leaves 22 to be subtracted by 6

Step 4: Decompose 22 into 1 ten and 2 ones

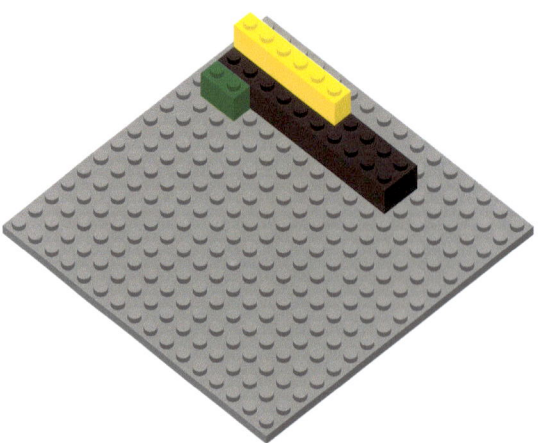

Step 5: Subtract 6 ones from 12 ones, leaving 6 ones and 1 ten. 32 – 16 = 16

**3.** Can you work with a partner to build a model to show this math sentence? 23 studs – 15 studs = ☐ studs

Show all the steps including the decomposing of the tens into ones.

How many studs are showing in your solution? _____

Draw the model of your solution. Explain how you found your solution.

*Possible solution:*

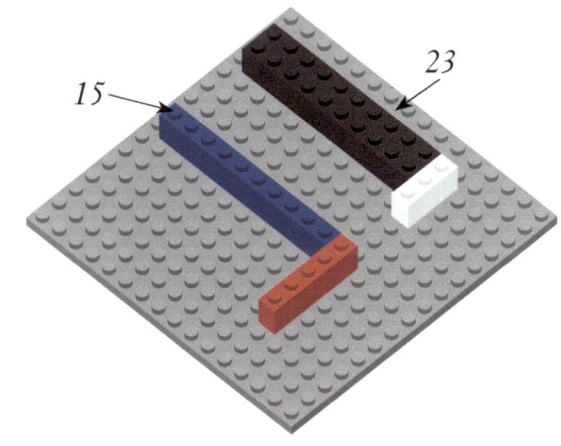

*Decomposing tens into ones*

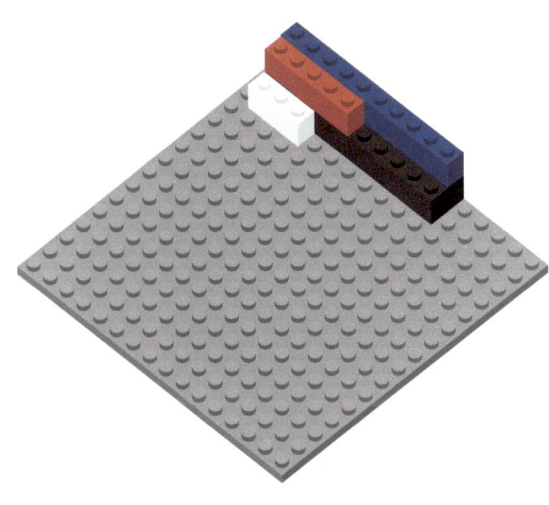

*8 studs showing*
*23 – 15 = 8*

DR. SHIRLEY DISSELER | TEACHING SUBTRACTION USING LEGO® BRICKS

## Challenge:

Build a model of two numbers and share it with a partner. Solve your partner's problem. Draw your partner's problem and solution.

*Solutions will vary.*

# RESULT UNKNOWN PROBLEMS WITHIN 20

### Students will learn/discover:
- How to represent and solve subtraction problems that are missing the difference
- How to write mathematical equations for models

### Why is this important?
Being able to represent and solve problems with missing parts in different locations helps students begin to understand the part-part-whole relationships between numbers. They learn to recognize the relationship between addition sums and subtraction differences as opposite.

### Vocabulary:
- Result unknown: Missing difference term in a subtraction problem
- Minuend: Largest number (and usually the first number) in a subtraction problem; the number that the subtrahend is subtracting from
- Subtrahend: Smaller of two numbers (and usually the second number) in a subtraction problem; the number that is being subtracted from the minuend
- Difference: Solution to a subtraction problem
- Minus: Symbol in a subtraction problem
- Subtract: Move from the whole
- Take Away: Move from the whole

## SUGGESTED BRICKS

| Size | Number |
|---|---|
| 1x1 | 10 each of 4 colors |
| 1x2 | 6 |
| 1x3 | 6 |
| 1x4 | 6 |
| 1x10 | 6 |
| 2x2 | 6 |
| 2x3 | 6 |
| 2x4 | 6 |

Note: Using a baseplate will help keep the bricks in a uniform line. One baseplate is suggested for these activities.

Note: The bricks used in these exercises may vary depending on how students are able to count. For example, if students can see that the 1x3 brick is the same as three 1x1 bricks, they may use that brick to show the number 3.

**How to use the companion student book, *Learning Subtraction Using LEGO® Bricks*:**
- After students build their models, have them draw the models and explain their thinking in the student book. Recording the models on paper after building them with bricks helps reinforce the concepts being taught.
- Discuss the vocabulary for each lesson with students as they work through the student book.
- Use the assessment in the student book to gauge student understanding of the content.

## Part 1: Show Them How

There are two different methods to model the solution of result unknown problems: the comparison method and the counting on method. Examples are included for each. *Note*: Although 1x10 strips are used here to model the comparison method and ten-frames are used here to model the counting on method, the 1x10 bricks and ten-frames are interchangeable as ways to show 10. Some students may not be developmentally ready to use 1x10 strips, so choose according to students' needs.

**Problem #1:** 7 – 3 = ☐

Be sure to discuss the vocabulary terms *minuend*, *subtrahend*, *difference*, and *result unknown*.

Ask students how to find the missing number (*difference*) that belongs in the box.

### Comparison method (using three 1x10 strips):
Build three 1x10 strips to represent the three numbers in the problem (the *minuend*, *subtrahend*, and *difference*).

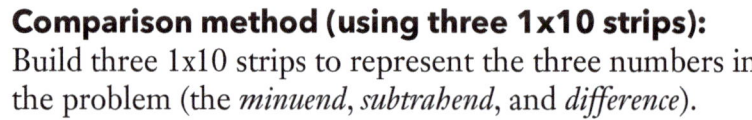

Place seven 1x1 bricks on the left strip to represent the *minuend* in the starting place. Place three 1x1 bricks on the center strip to represent the *subtrahend* in the change location. Do not place any studs on the right strip to represent the *difference*, which is unknown.

Ask students how to determine the missing number using subtraction strategies. Students could use strategies like counting up, one-to-one correspondence, part-part-whole, or matching to find the solution.

Have students put a finger on top of the 1x10 strip that shows the number being taken away or subtracted (the center strip). Use the vocabulary (the *subtrahend*). Count the number of studs on that strip using one-to-one correspondence. Explain that this number is in the change location and is the number that the minuend has to be reduced by to determine the difference or result unknown. Have students place the 3 studs from this strip on top of the 7 studs on the left strip that represent the minuend to find the difference. Students should compare to find 4 uncovered studs.

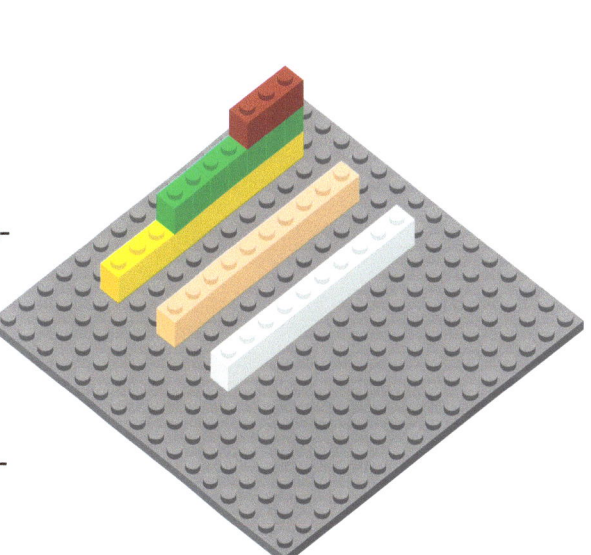

Have students model all the parts of the problem with 7 studs on the left strip (*minuend*), 3 studs on the center strip (*subtrahend*), and 4 studs on the right strip (*difference*). Ask students if they notice anything interesting in the model. Students should see that the studs on the right strip added to the studs on the center strip are equivalent to the studs on the left strip. Students who understand this are beginning to see the link between addition and subtraction.

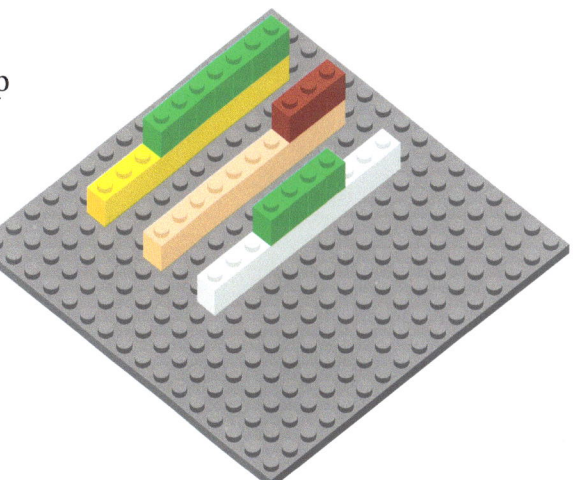

Have students draw the model, explain the parts of the problem, and write the math sentence. Students should be able to explain that the start number or minuend is 7 and the change number or subtrahend is 3. Covering the 7 studs on the left strip with 3 studs from the center strip leaves 4 studs uncovered. This shows the result unknown or difference of 4. Some students may understand that they can use addition to check by working backwards. 7 – 4 = 3

**Counting on method (using one ten-frame):**
Review of ten-frames: If students have not used ten-frames recently, review the strategy at the beginning of Chapter 2.

Build one ten-frame. Use either one 2x4 brick and one 1x2 brick of the same color, or use one 2x3 brick and one 2x2 brick of the same color.

Place 7 studs on the ten-frame. Choose 3 studs of another color.

Place those 3 studs on top of the 7 studs that are on the ten-frame. Ask students what the 3 studs show. Students should understand that 3 is the subtrahend or the amount being subtracted in the problem. They may say 3 is the answer, but it is not. The answer to the problem is 4.

Have students count on from the 3 studs to the original 7 ("4, 5, 6, 7"). Ask them how many studs they counted on. Students should understand they have counted on 4 more studs, which is the *difference*.

Have students draw the model, explain the parts of the problem, and write the math sentence. Students should be able to explain that the start number is 7. Placing 3 studs from the subtrahend on top of the minuend's 7 studs and counting up to 7 shows 4 studs, which is the difference or result unknown. 7 – 3 = 4

## Result Unknown Problem #2: 9 – 5 = ☐

**Comparison method (using 1x10 strips):**
Build three 1x10 strips to represent the three numbers in the problem (the *minuend*, *subtrahend*, and *difference*).

Place 9 studs on the left strip to represent the minuend in the starting place.

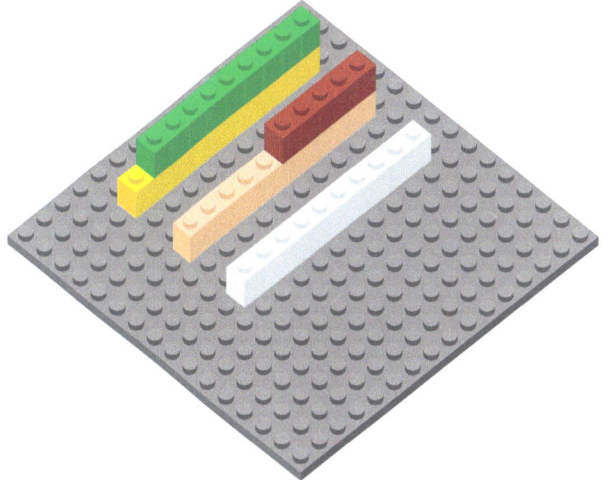

Place 5 studs on the center strip to represent the subtrahend or the amount being subtracted.

Do not place any studs on the right strip to represent the difference or result unknown.

Ask students how to determine the missing number using subtraction strategies. Students could use strategies like counting up, one-to-one correspondence, part-part-whole, or matching to find the solution.

Have students put a finger on the center 1x10 strip that shows the number being taken away or subtracted. Use the vocabulary (*subtrahend*). Count the number of studs on that strip using one-to-one correspondence. Explain that this number (5) is in the change location and is the number that the minuend has to be reduced by to determine the difference or result unknown. Have students place these 5 studs on top of the 9 studs that represent the minuend on the left strip to find the difference. Students should compare to find 4 uncovered studs.

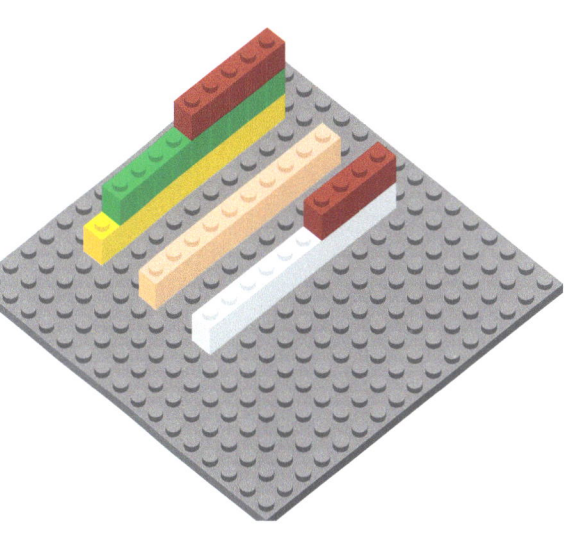

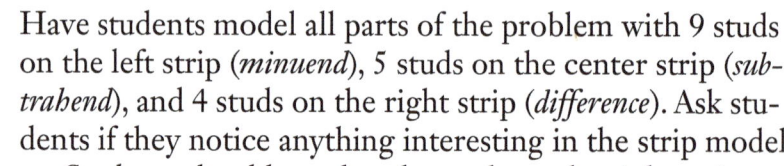

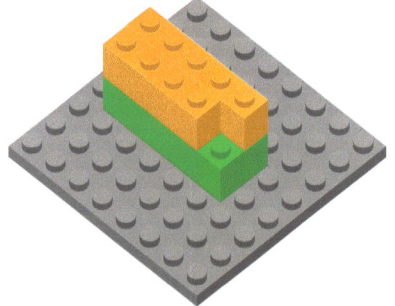

Have students model all parts of the problem with 9 studs on the left strip (*minuend*), 5 studs on the center strip (*subtrahend*), and 4 studs on the right strip (*difference*). Ask students if they notice anything interesting in the strip model. Students should see that the studs on the right strip added to the studs on the center strip are equivalent to the studs on the left strip. Students who understand this are beginning to see the link between addition and subtraction.

Have students draw the model, explain the parts of the problem, and write the math sentence.

Students should be able to explain that the start number or minuend is 9 and the change number or subtrahend is 5. Covering the 9 studs on the left strip with 5 studs from the center strip leaves 4 studs uncovered. This shows the result unknown or difference of 4. Some students may understand that they can use addition to check by working backwards. 9 – 5 = 4

### Counting on method (using one ten-frame):
Build one ten-frame.

Place 9 studs on the ten-frame. Choose 5 studs of another color.

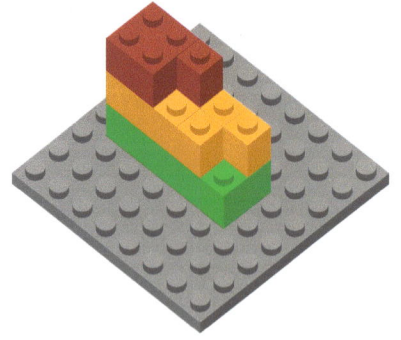

Have students place those 5 studs on top of the 9 studs that are on the ten-frame. Ask students what the 5 studs show. Students should understand that 5 is the subtrahend or the amount being subtracted in the problem. They may say 5 is the answer, but it is not. The answer to the problem is 4.

Have students count on from the 5 studs to the original 9 ("6, 7, 8, 9"). Ask them how many studs they counted on. Students should understand they have counted on 4 more studs, which is the *difference*.

Have students draw the model, explain the parts of the problem, and write the math sentence. Students should be able to explain that the start number is 9. Placing 5 studs from the subtrahend on top of the minuend's 9 studs and counting up to 9 shows 5 studs, which is the difference or result unknown.

## Problem #3: 8 – 2 = ☐

**Comparison method (using three 1x10 strips):**
Build three 1x10 strips to represent the problem.

Place 8 studs on the left strip to represent the minuend in the starting place.

Place 2 studs on the center strip to represent the subtrahend or the amount being subtracted.

Do not place any studs on the right strip to represent the difference or result unknown.

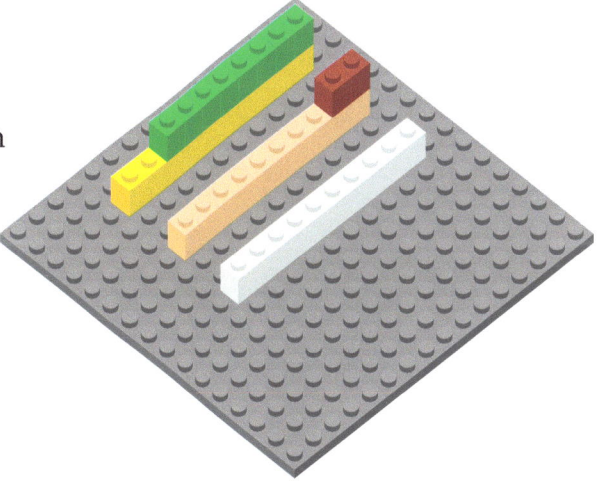

Ask students how to determine the missing number using subtraction strategies. Students could use strategies like counting up, one-to-one correspondence, part-part-whole, or matching to find the solution.

Have students put a finger on the center 1x10 strip that shows the number being taken away or subtracted. Use the vocabulary (*subtrahend*). Count the number of studs on that strip using one-to-one correspondence. Explain that this number (2) is in the change location and is the number that the minuend has to be reduced by to determine the difference or result unknown. Have students place these 2 studs on top of the 8 studs that represent the minuend on the left strip to find the difference. Students should compare to find 6 uncovered studs.

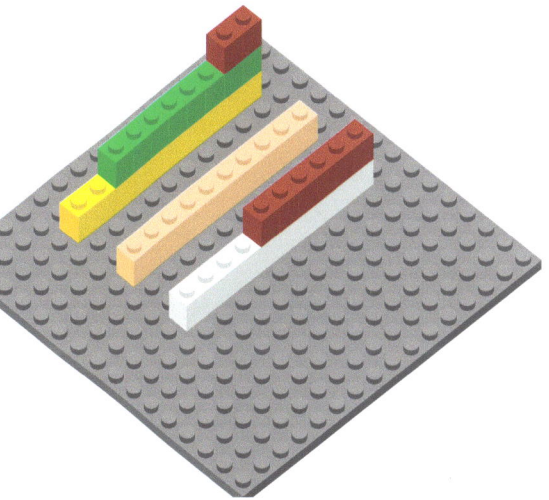

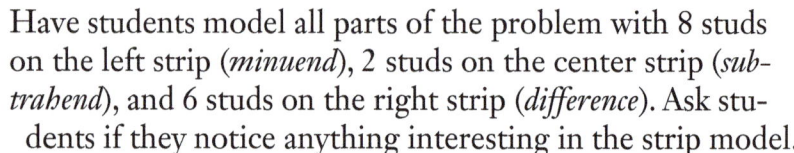

Have students model all parts of the problem with 8 studs on the left strip (*minuend*), 2 studs on the center strip (*subtrahend*), and 6 studs on the right strip (*difference*). Ask students if they notice anything interesting in the strip model. Students should see that the studs on the right strip added to the studs on the center strip are equivalent to the studs on the left strip. Students who understand this are beginning to see the link between addition and subtraction.

Have students draw the model, explain the parts of the problem, and write the math sentence. Students should be able to explain that the start number or minuend is 8 and the change number or subtrahend is 2. Covering the 8 studs on the left strip with 2 studs from the center strip leaves 6 studs uncovered. This shows the result unknown or difference of 6. Some students may understand that they can use addition to check by working backwards. 8 – 2 = 6

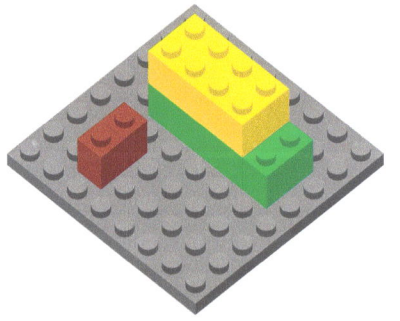

**Counting on method (using one ten-frame):**
Build one ten-frame.

Place 8 studs on the ten-frame. Choose 2 studs of another color.

Have students place those 2 studs on top of the 8 studs that are on the ten-frame. Ask students what the 2 studs show. Students should understand that 2 is the subtrahend or the amount being subtracted in the problem. They may say 2 is the answer, but it is not. The answer to the problem is 6.

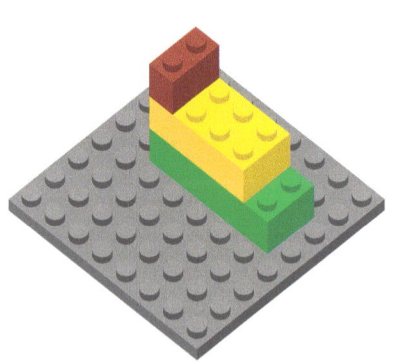

Have students count on from the 2 studs to the original 8 ("3, 4, 5, 6, 7, 8"). Ask them how many studs they counted on. Students should understand they have counted on 6 more studs, which is the *difference*.

Have students draw the model, explain the parts of the problem, and write the math sentence. Students should be able to explain that the start number is 8. Placing 2 studs from the subtrahend on top of the minuend's 8 studs and counting up to 8 shows 6 studs, which is the difference or result unknown.

## Part 2: Show What You Know

**1.** Can you build a model that shows this math sentence?

5 – 3 = ☐

You can use a 1x10 strip model or a ten-frame model. Draw your model.

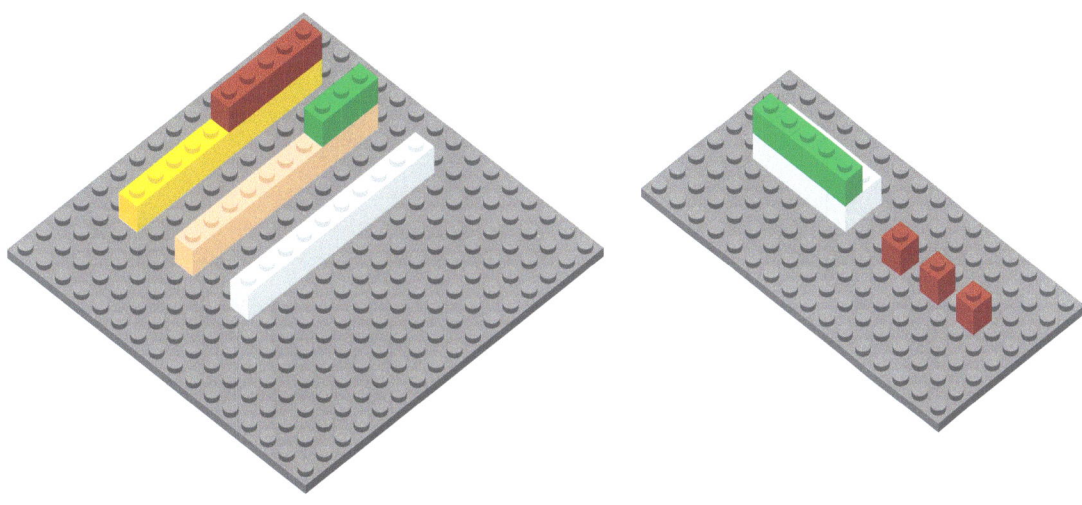

Model the result unknown and explain how you found the difference. Draw all three parts of the problem. Label the *minuend*, the *subtrahend*, and the *difference*.

*Answer*: In the 1x10 strip model, the comparison is being made between the 5 studs from the left strip and the 2 studs from the center strip. In the ten-frame model, 2 studs are uncovered, which is the result unknown or difference.

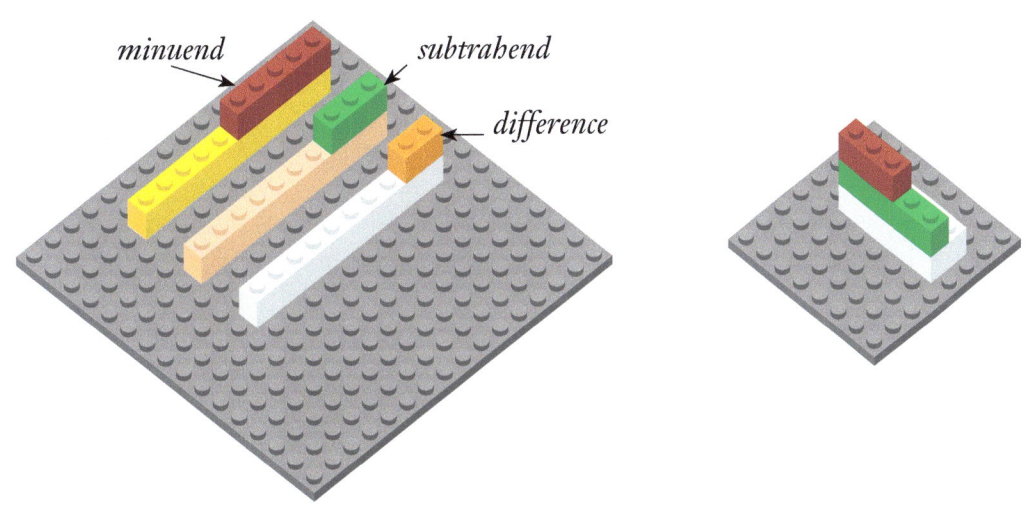

**2.** Can you build a model that shows this math sentence?

10 − 7 = ☐

You can use a 1x10 strip model or a ten-frame model. Draw your model.

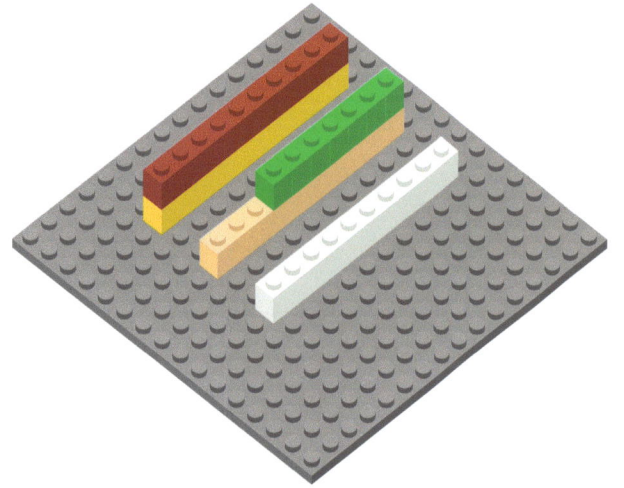
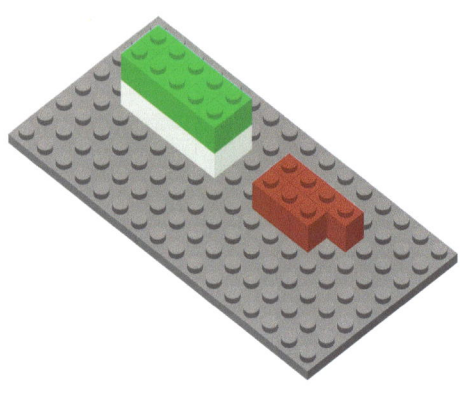

Model the result unknown and explain how you found the difference. Draw all three parts of the problem. Label the *minuend*, the *subtrahend*, and the *difference*.

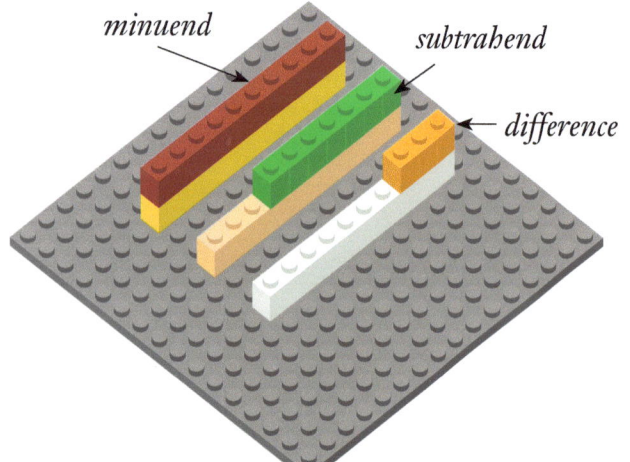
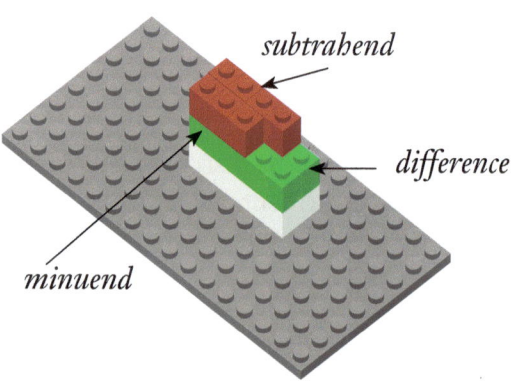

*Answer*: In the 1x10 strip model, the comparison is being made between the 10 studs from the left strip and the 7 studs from the center strip. In the ten-frame model, 3 studs are uncovered, which is the result unknown or difference.

**3.** Can you build a model that shows this math sentence?

6 − 3 = ☐

You can use a 1x10 strip model or a ten-frame model. Draw your model.

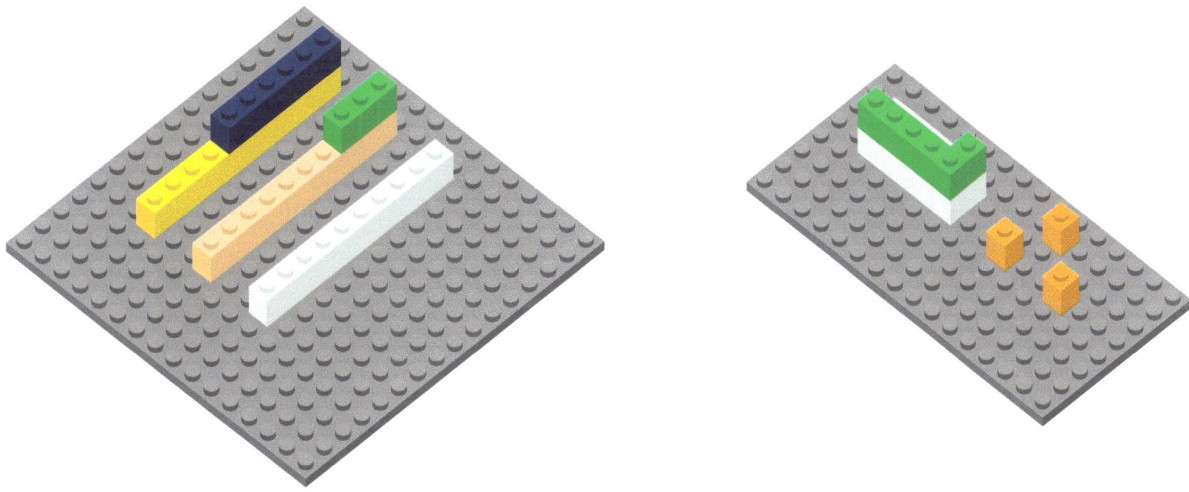

Model the result unknown and explain how you found the difference. Draw all three parts of the problem. Label the *minuend*, the *subtrahend*, and the *difference*.

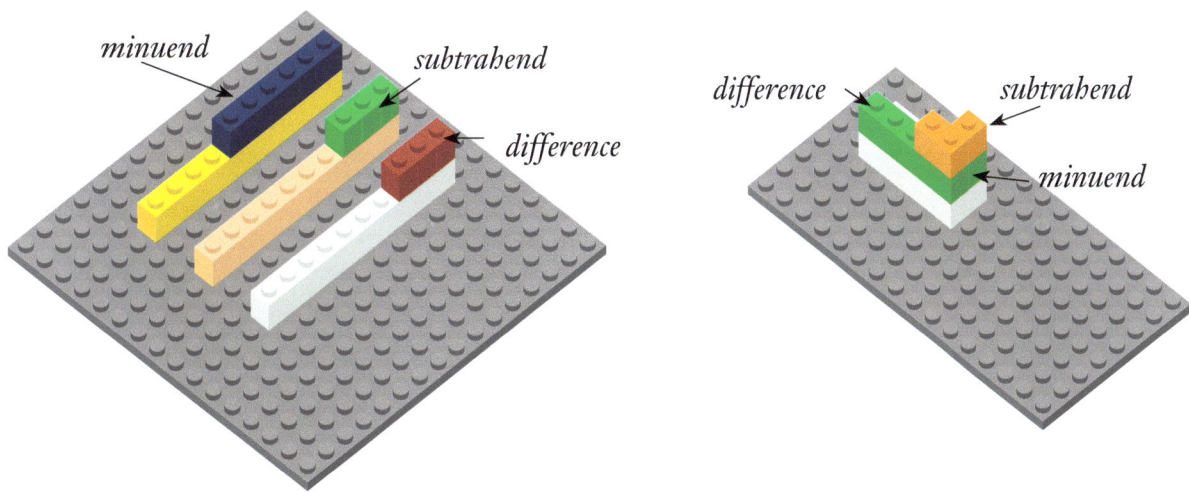

*Answer*: In the 1x10 strip model, the comparison is being made between the 6 studs from the left strip and the 3 studs from the center strip. In the ten-frame model, 3 studs are uncovered, which is the result unknown or difference.

## Challenge:

Can you build a model that shows this math sentence?

12 − 7 = ☐

*Hint:* Use two 1x10 strips or two ten-frames to model 12.

Build a model of your solution. Draw your solution model. Explain your solution.

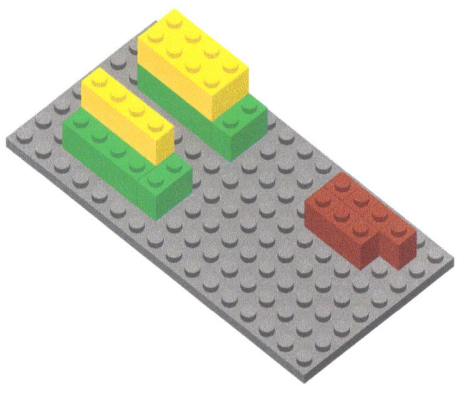

12 − 7 = ☐

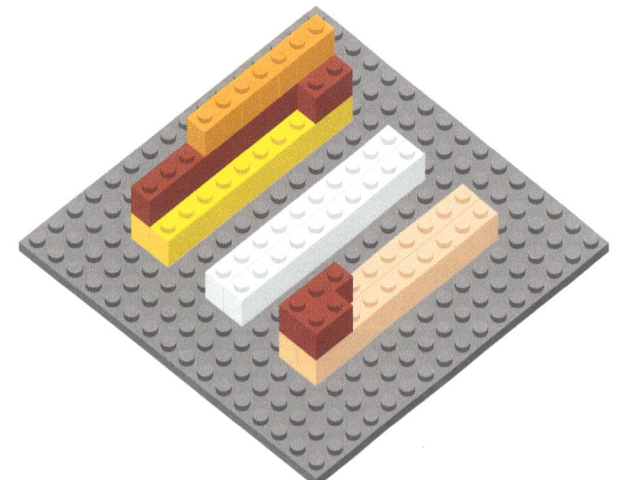
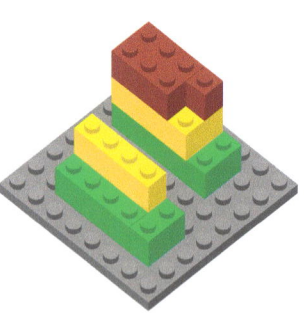

*5 studs uncovered is difference (result unknown) of 5*

*Note*: Students can stack 12 on the left strip to show 12 rather than using two 1x10 strips.

# CHANGE UNKNOWN PROBLEMS WITHIN 20

### SUGGESTED BRICKS

| Size | Number |
|---|---|
| 1x1 | 10 each of 4 colors |
| 1x2 | 6 |
| 1x3 | 6 |
| 1x4 | 6 |
| 1x10 | 6 |
| 2x2 | 6 |
| 2x3 | 6 |
| 2x4 | 6 |

Note: Using a baseplate will help keep the bricks in a uniform line. One baseplate is suggested for these activities.

Note: The bricks used in these exercises may vary depending upon how students are able to count. For example, if students can see that the 1x3 brick is the same as three 1x1 bricks, they may use the 1x3 brick to show the number 3.

### Students will learn/discover:
- How to solve subtraction problems where the number in the change location is unknown
- How to write mathematical equations for models

### Why is this important?
Understanding subtraction problems with missing terms in different locations is important for students to make sense of the part-part-whole relationships between numbers. Solving change unknown problems helps students connect the opposite relationship between addition and subtraction.

### Vocabulary:
- Change unknown: Missing subtrahend in a subtraction problem, or the amount by which the start number in a subtraction problem is changed
- Minuend: Largest number (and usually the first number) in a subtraction problem; the number that the subtrahend is subtracting from
- Subtrahend: Smaller of two numbers (and usually the second number) in a subtraction problem; the number that is being subtracted from the minuend
- Difference: Solution to a subtraction problem
- Minus: Symbol in a subtraction problem
- Subtract: Move from the whole
- Take Away: Move from the whole

**How to use the companion student book,** *Learning Subtraction Using LEGO® Bricks*:
- After students build their models, have them draw the models and explain their thinking in the student book. Recording the models on paper after building them with bricks helps reinforce the concepts being taught.
- Discuss the vocabulary for each lesson with students as they work through the student book.
- Use the assessment in the student book to gauge student understanding of the content.

## Part 1: Show Them How

There are two different methods to model the solution of result unknown problems: the comparison method and the counting on method. Examples are included for each. *Note*: Although 1x10 strips are used here to model the comparison method and ten-frames are used here to model the counting on method, the 1x10 bricks and ten-frames are interchangeable as ways to show 10. Some students may not be developmentally ready for using 1x10 strips, so choose according to students' needs.

## Problem #1: $7 - \boxed{\phantom{x}} = 4$

Be sure to discuss the vocabulary terms *minuend*, *subtrahend*, *difference*, and *change unknown*.

Ask students how to find the missing number (*subtrahend*) that belongs in the box.

### Comparision method (using three 1x10 strips):
Build three 1x10 strips to represent the three numbers in the problem (the *minuend*, *subtrahend*, and *difference*).

Place seven 1x1 bricks on the left strip to represent the *minuend* in the starting place. Do not place any studs on the center strip to represent the *subtrahend* in the change location, which is unknown. Place four 1x1 bricks on the right strip to represent the *difference*.

Ask students how to determine the missing number using subtraction strategies. Students could use strategies like counting up, one-to-one correspondence, part-part-whole, or matching to find the solution.

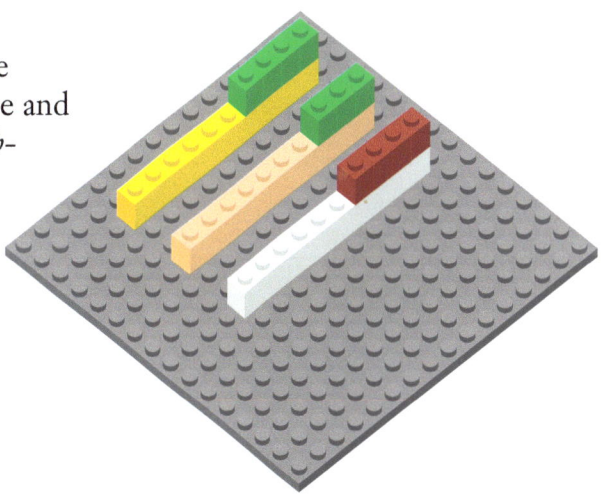

Ask students how many studs they have to remove from the left strip to make it the same length as the right strip. (3) Have students remove 3 studs from the left strip and place them on the center strip.

Show that the left and right strips now have the same number of studs by using one-to-one correspondence and counting. Explain that the number in the middle (*subtrahend*) is in the change unknown location. It is the number that the *minuend* has to be changed by to determine the *difference* of 4.

**4.** Have students model all the parts of the problem by placing the 3 studs back on the left strip to total 7 studs and placing 3 studs of another color on the center strip. Ask students if they notice anything interesting in the model. Students should answer that the studs on the right strip added to the studs on the center strip are equivalent to the studs on the left strip. Students who understand this are beginning to see the link between addition and subtraction.

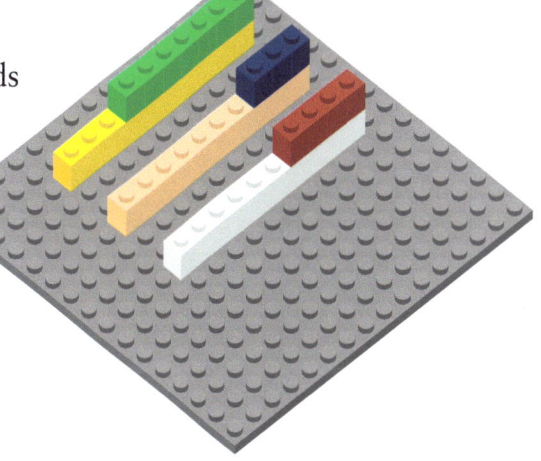

**5.** Have students draw the model, explain the parts of the problem, and write the math sentence. Students should be able to explain that the start number is 7. Comparing the 7 studs on the left strip to the 4 studs on the right strip shows that the missing subtrahend or change unknown number is 3. Some students may understand that they can use addition to check by working backwards. 7 – 3 = 4

### Counting on method (using one ten-frame):

Review of ten-frames: If students have not used ten-frames recently, review the strategy at the beginning of Chapter 2.

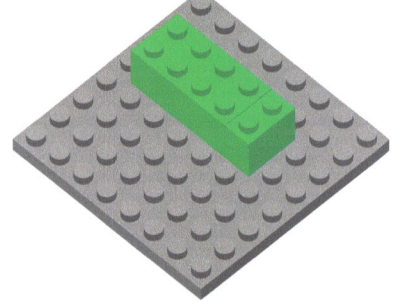

Build one ten-frame. Use either one 2x4 brick and one 1x2 brick of the same color, or use one 2x3 brick and one 2x2 brick of the same color.

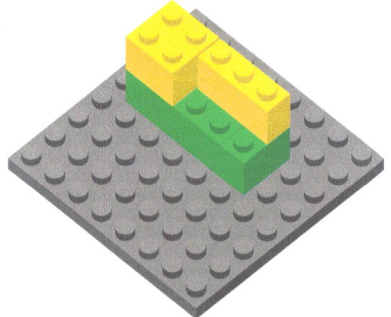

Place 7 studs on the ten-frame.

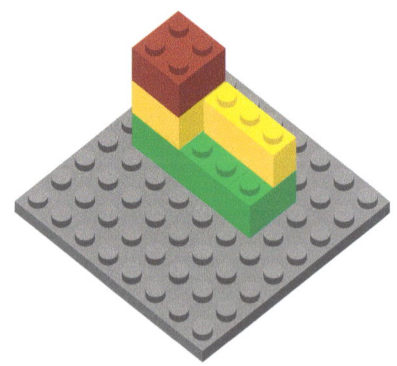

Ask students to choose 4 studs of another color and place them on top of the 7 studs. Ask students what the number 4 means in this problem. Students should understand that 4 is the difference in the problem. They may say it is the answer, but it is not. The answer to the problem is 3.

Ask students how many studs are left uncovered. Have students count on from the 4 studs to the start number of 7 ("5, 6, 7"). Ask them how many studs they counted on. Students should understand they have counted on 3 more studs, which is the *change unknown* number or the *subtrahend*. Ask students the solution to the problem. (3 studs)

Have students draw the model, explain the parts of the problem, and write the math sentence. Students should be able to explain that the start number is 7. Placing 4 studs from the difference on top of the minuend's 7 studs and counting up to 7 shows 3 studs, which is the subtrahend or change unknown.  7 – 3 = 4

## Problem #2: 9 – ☐ = 5

**Comparision method (using three 1x10 strips):**
Build three 1x10 strips to represent the three numbers in the problem (the *minuend*, *subtrahend*, and *difference*).

Place 9 studs on the left strip to represent the minuend in the starting place. Do not place any studs on the center strip to represent the missing subtrahend or the change unknown. Place 5 studs on the right strip to represent the difference.

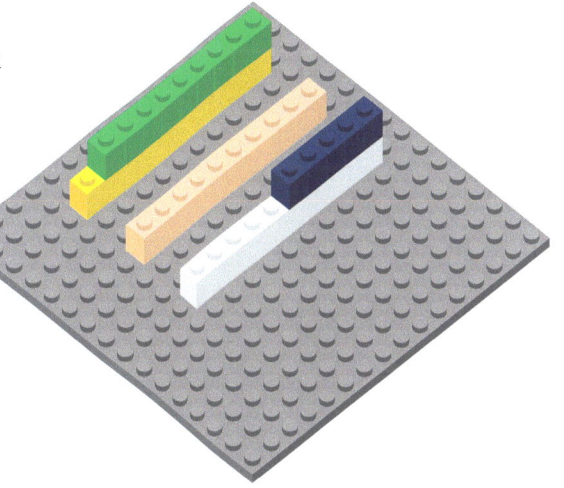

Ask students how to determine the missing number using subtraction strategies. Students could use strategies like counting on, one-to-one correspondence, part-part-whole, or matching to find the solution.

Ask students how many studs to remove from the left strip to make it the same length as the right strip. (4) Have students remove 4 studs from the left strip and place them on the center strip.

Show that the left and right strips now have the same number of studs by using one-to-one correspondence and counting. Explain that the number in the middle (subtrahend) is in the change unknown location. It is the number that the minuend has to be changed by to determine the difference of 5.

Model all the parts of the problem by placing the 4 studs back on the left strip and placing 4 studs of another color on the center strip. Ask students if they notice anything interesting in the model. Students should answer that the studs on the right strip added to the studs on the center strip are equivalent to the studs on the left strip. Students who understand this are beginning to see the link between addition and subtraction.

Have students draw the model, explain the parts of the problem, and write the math sentence. Students should be able to explain that the start number is 9. Comparing the 9 studs on the left strip to the 5 studs on the right strip shows that the missing subtrahend or change unknown number is 4. Some students may understand that they can use addition to check by working backwards. 9 – 4 = 5

**Counting on method (using one ten-frame):**
Build one ten-frame.

Place 9 studs on the ten-frame.

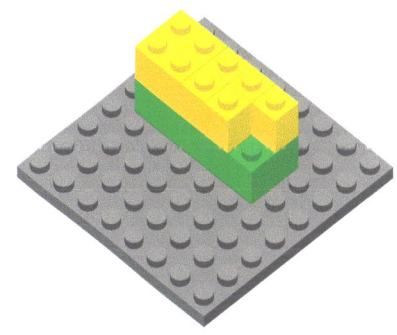

Ask students to choose 5 studs of another color and place them on top of the 9 studs. Ask students what the number 5 means in this problem. Students should understand that 5 is the difference in the problem. They may say it is the answer, but it is not. The answer to the problem is 4.

Ask students how many studs are left uncovered. Have students count on from the 5 studs to the original 9 ("6, 7, 8, 9"). Ask them how many studs they counted on. Students should understand they have counted on 4 more studs, which is the *change unknown* number or the *subtrahend*. Ask students the solution to the problem. (4 studs)

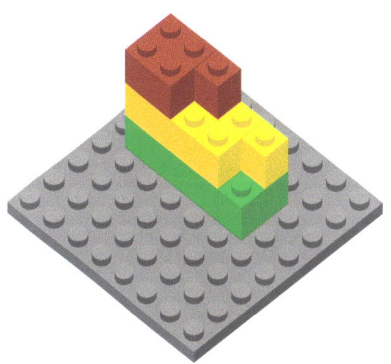

Have students draw the model, explain the parts of the problem, and write the math sentence. Students should be able to explain that the start number is 9. Placing 5 studs from the difference on top of the minuend's 9 studs and counting up to 9 shows 4 studs, which is the subtrahend or change unknown.  $9 - 4 = 5$

# Problem #3: $8 - \boxed{\phantom{0}} = 2$

**Comparison model (using three 1x10 strips):**
Build three 1x10 number strips to represent the three numbers in the problem (the *minuend*, *subtrahend*, and *difference*).

Place 8 studs on the left strip to represent the minuend in the starting place. Do not place any studs on the center strip to represent the missing subtrahend or the change unknown. Place 2 studs on the right strip to represent the difference.

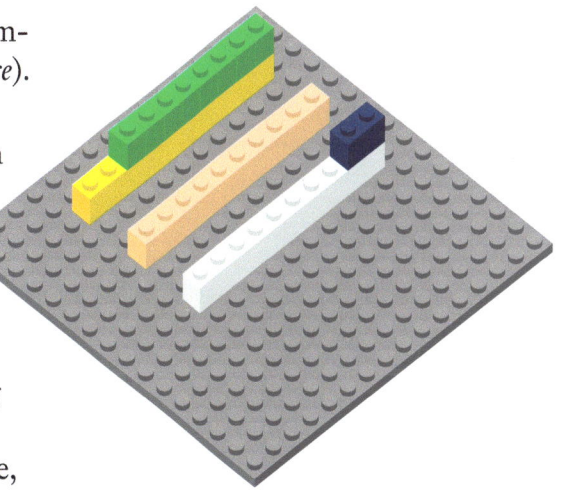

Ask students how to determine the missing number using subtraction strategies. Students could use strategies like counting on, one-to-one correspondence, part-part-whole, or matching to find the solution.

Ask students how many studs they have to remove from the left strip to make it the same length as the right strip. (6) Have students remove 6 studs from the left strip and place them on the center strip.

Model all the parts of the problem by placing the 6 studs back on the left strip and placing 6 studs of another color on the center strip. Ask students if they notice anything interesting in the model. Students should answer that the studs on the right strip added to the studs on the center strip are equivalent to the studs on the left strip. Students who understand this are beginning to see the link between addition and subtraction.

Have students draw the model, explain the parts of the problem, and write the math sentence. Students should be able to explain that the start number is 8. Comparing the 8 studs on the left strip to the 2 studs on the right strip shows that the missing subtrahend or change unknown number is 6. Some students may understand that they can use addition to check by working backwards. 8 – 6 = 2

**Counting on method (using one ten-frame):**
Build one ten-frame.

Place 8 studs on the ten-frame.

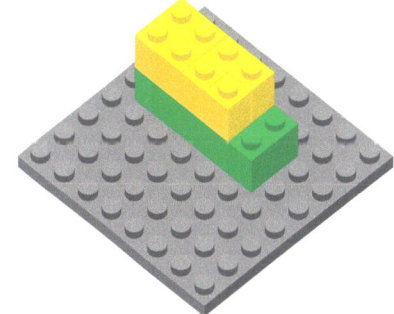

Ask students to choose 2 studs of another color and place them on top of the 8 studs. Ask students what the number 2 means in this problem. Students should understand that 2 is the difference in the problem. They may say it is the answer, but it is not. The answer to the problem is 6.

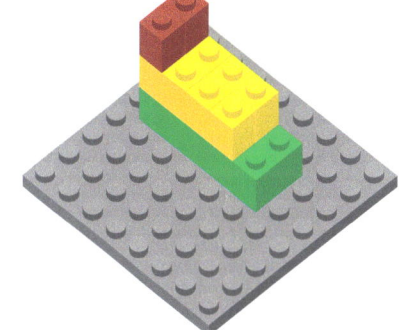

Ask students how many studs are left uncovered. Have students count on from the 2 studs to the original 8 ("3, 4, 5, 6, 7, 8"). Ask them how many studs they counted on. Students should understand they have counted on 6 more studs, which is the *change unknown* number or the *subtrahend*. Ask students the solution to the problem. (6 studs)

Have students draw the model, explain the parts of the problem, and write the math sentence. Students should be able to explain that the start number is 8. Placing 2 studs from the difference on top of the minuend's 8 studs and counting up to 8 shows 6 studs, which is the subtrahend or change unknown.  $8 - 6 = 2$

## Part 2: Show What You Know

**1.** Can you build a model that shows this math sentence?

5 − ☐ = 3

You can use a 1x10 strip model or a ten-frame model. Draw your model.

Model the missing subtrahend. Draw all three parts of the problem. Label the *minuend*, *subtrahend*, and *difference*. Explain how you found the missing term.

*Answer*: Using the 1x10 strip model, the 2 studs on the center strip represent the change needed to make the left and right strips equivalent. Using the ten-frame model, there are 2 studs uncovered, representing the change unknown number or missing subtrahend.

*Suggested models:*

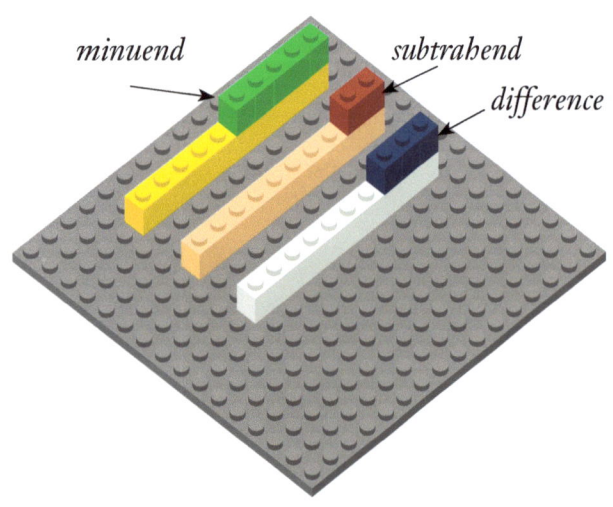
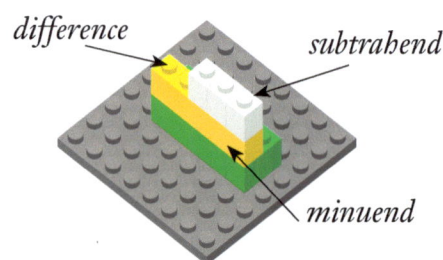

**60** TEACHING SUBTRACTION USING LEGO® BRICKS | DR. SHIRLEY DISSELER

**2.** Can you build a model that shows this math sentence?

10 − ☐ = 4

You can use a 1x10 strip model or a ten-frame model. Draw your model.

Model the missing subtrahend. Draw all three parts of the problem. Label the *minuend*, *subtrahend*, and *difference*. Explain how you found the missing term.

*Answer*: Using the 1x10 strip model, the 6 studs on the center strip represent the change needed to make the left and right strips equivalent. Using the ten-frame model, there are 6 studs uncovered, representing the missing subtrahend.

*Suggested models:*

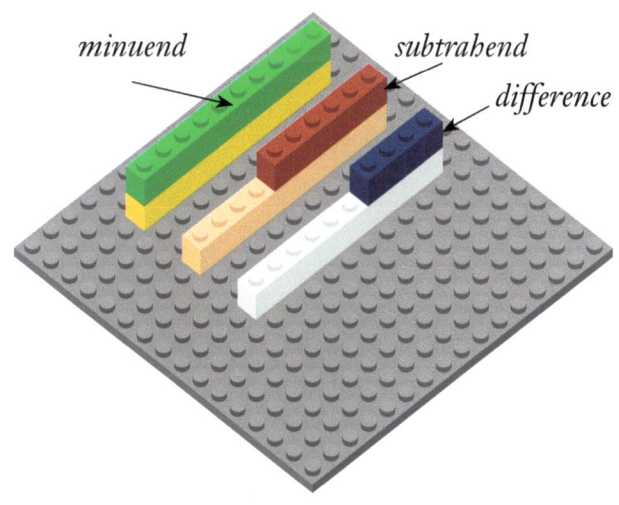
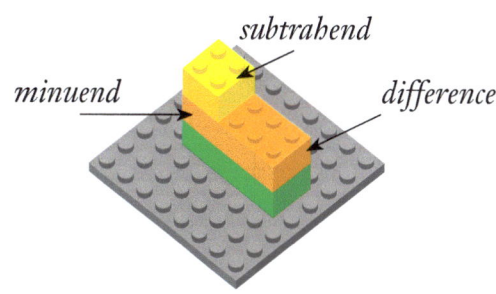

**3.** Can you build a model that shows this math sentence?

7 − ☐ = 5

You can use a 1 x 10 strip model or a ten-frame model. Draw your model.

Model the missing subtrahend. Draw all three parts of the problem. Label the *minuend*, *subtrahend*, and *difference*. Explain how you found the missing term.

*Answer*: Using the 1x10 strip model, the 2 studs on the center strip represent the change needed to make the left and right strips equivalent. Using the ten-frame model, there are 2 studs uncovered, representing the missing subtrahend.

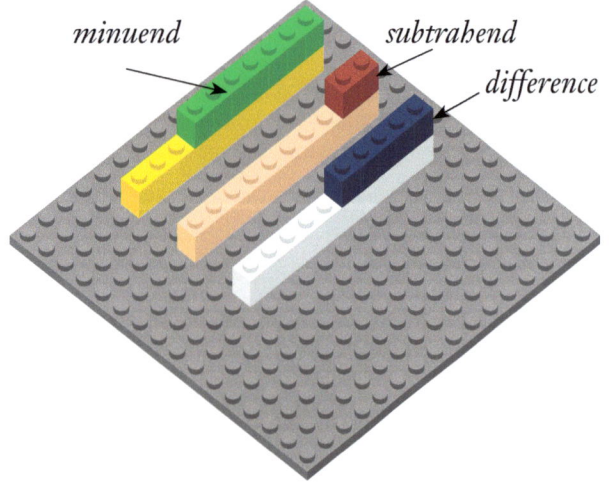

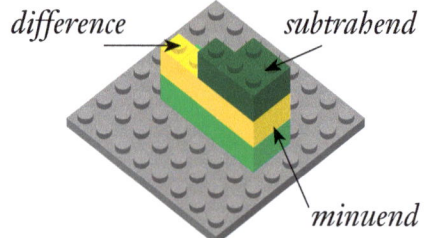

## Challenge:

Can you build a model to show this problem? 12 – ☐ = 7

Draw a solution for your model to show the change unknown number. Explain your solution.

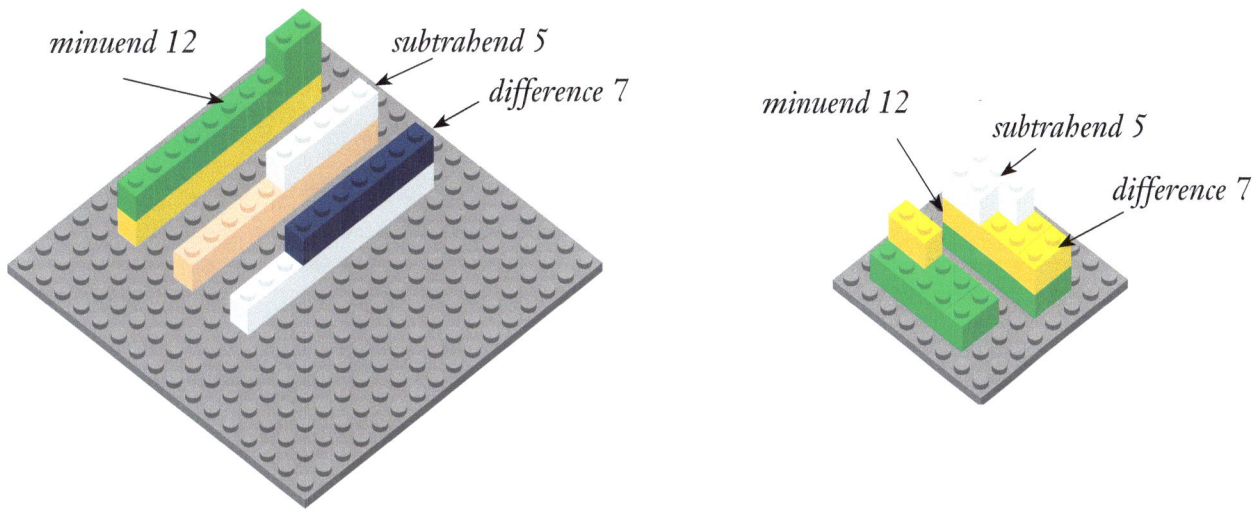

*Note*: To model 12, students can stack 12 studs on the 1x10 strip or build two ten-frames.

# 7

## SUGGESTED BRICKS

| Size | Number |
|---|---|
| 1x1 | 10 each of 4 colors |
| 1x2 | 6 |
| 1x3 | 6 |
| 1x4 | 6 |
| 1x10 | 6 |
| 2x2 | 6 |
| 2x3 | 6 |
| 2x4 | 6 |

Note: Using a baseplate will help keep the bricks in a uniform line. One baseplate is suggested for these activities.

# START UNKNOWN PROBLEMS WITHIN 20

**Students will learn/discover:**
- How to solve subtraction problems where the starting number in the problem is unknown
- How to write mathematical equations for models

**Why is this important?**
Understanding subtraction problems with missing terms in different locations is important for students to make sense of the part-part-whole relationships between numbers. Having the unknown term at the start of the subtraction problem requires some abstract thinking to determine the difference. This skill serves as a stepping stone to math skills that go beyond subtraction. It will become important later as students move into pre-algebra and begin to use equations with variables.

**Vocabulary:**
- Start Unknown: beginning number (minuend) in a subtraction problem is missing
- Minuend: Largest number (and usually the first number) in a subtraction problem; the number that the subtrahend is subtracting from
- Subtrahend: Smaller of two numbers (and usually the second number) in a subtraction problem; the number that is being subtracted from the minuend
- Difference: Solution to a subtraction problem
- Minus: Symbol in a subtraction problem
- Subtract: Move from the whole
- Take Away: Move from the whole

**How to use the companion student book, *Learning Subtraction Using LEGO® Bricks*:**
- After students build their models, have them draw the models and explain their thinking in the student book. Recording the models on paper after building them with bricks helps reinforce the concepts being taught.
- Discuss the vocabulary for each lesson with students as they work through the student book.
- Use the assessment in the student book to gauge student understanding of the content.

## Part 1: Show Them How

### Review of ten-frames:
If students have not used ten-frames recently, review the strategy at the start of Chapter 2.

**1. Problem:** ☐ – 3 = 7

Ask students how to find the missing number (minuend) that belongs in the box.

Build three 1x10 strips or three ten-frames to represent the three numbers in the problem (*minuend*, *subtrahend*, and *difference*).

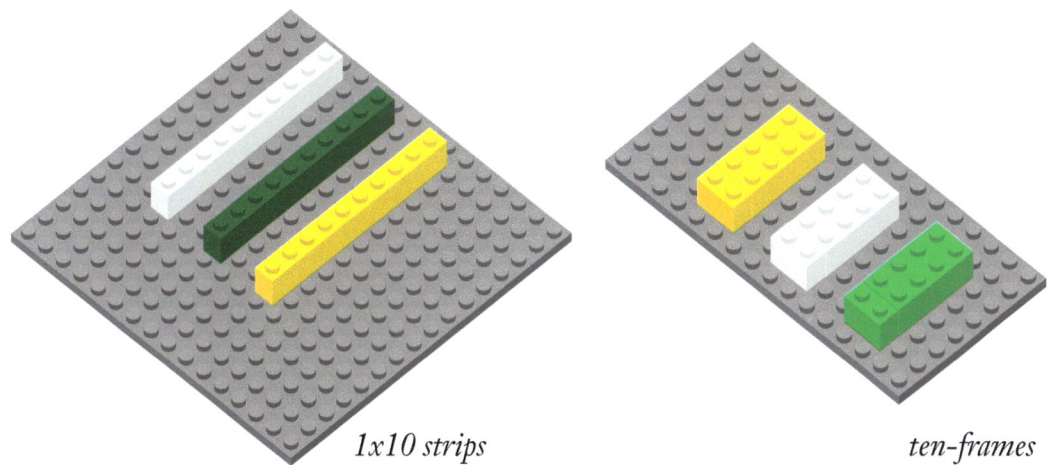

*1x10 strips*  *ten-frames*

**2.** Do not place any bricks on the left strip or ten-frame, since the box for the minuend in the math sentence is empty and still unknown. Place 3 studs on the center strip to represent the subtrahend 3 in the change location. Place 7 studs on right strip to represent the difference. Have students draw the model and write the math sentence it represents, which is ☐ – 3 = 7.

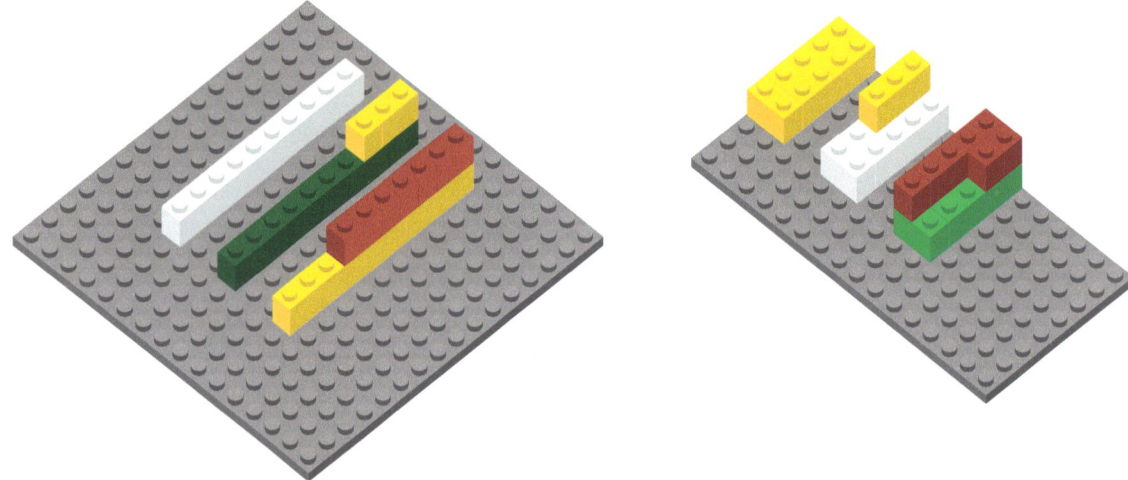

**3.** Ask students how to determine the starting number using subtraction strategies. Students could use strategies like counting up, one-to-one correspondence, part-part-whole, or matching to find the solution. Ask students if the start number should be larger or smaller than the difference, and help them understand why it should be larger.

Use *working backwards* as the solving strategy. Tell students that taking the parts and putting them together is a way to find the whole.

Move the 7 studs from the right strip (*difference*) to the starting location (*minuend*). Fill in the missing studs on the minuend strip with the 3 studs from the center strip (*subtrahend*). The total number of studs on the first strip now represents the start number of 10.

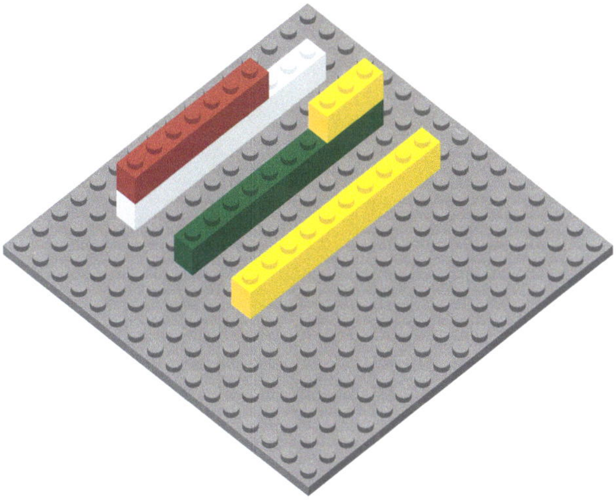

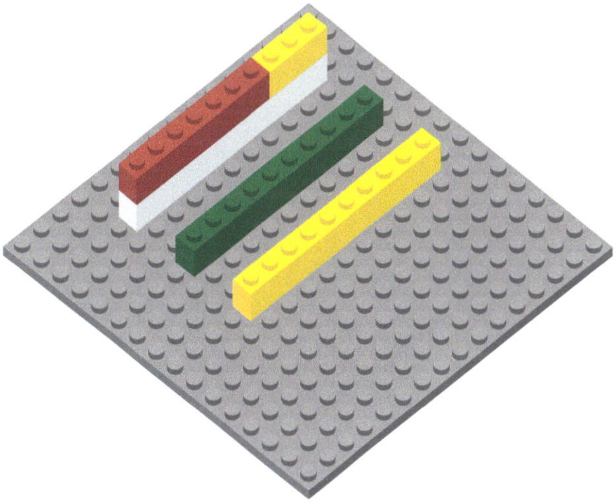

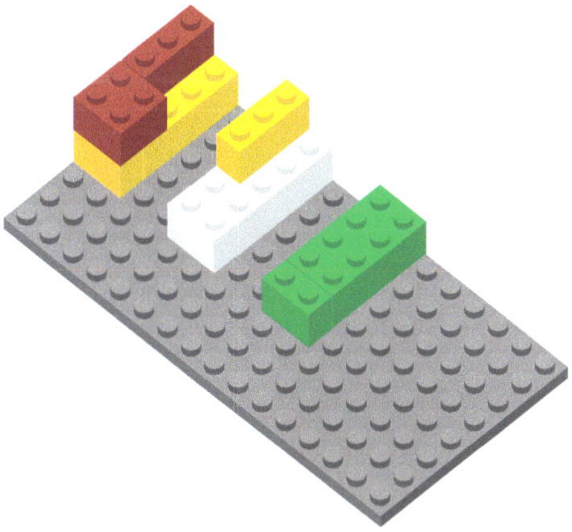

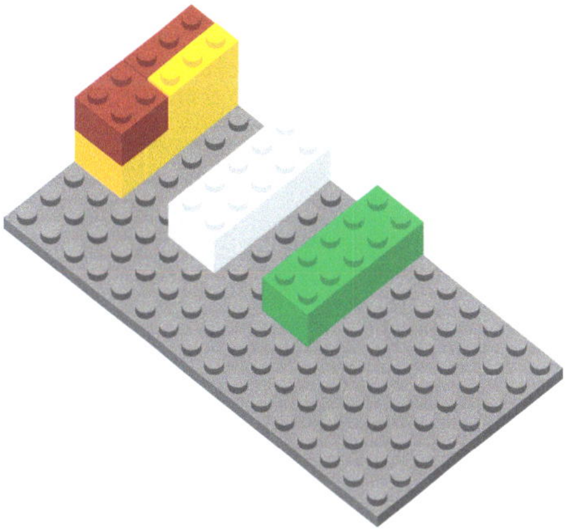

**4.** Show how to check this by taking 3 studs away from the 10 studs in the starting location and move them back to the center strip. Move 7 studs from the starting location to the difference location (the right strip). If the starting strip is now empty, the solution is correct.

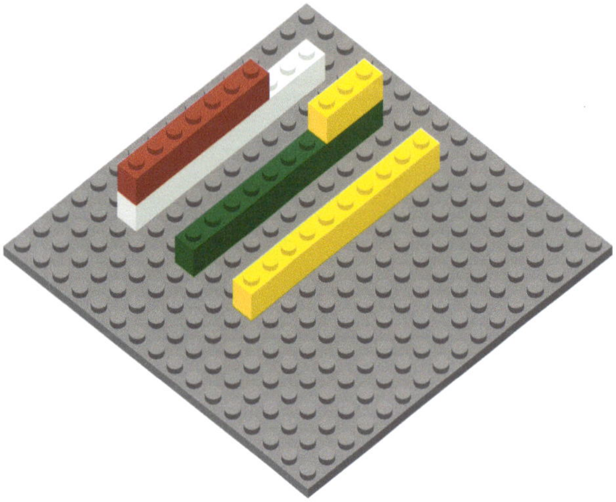

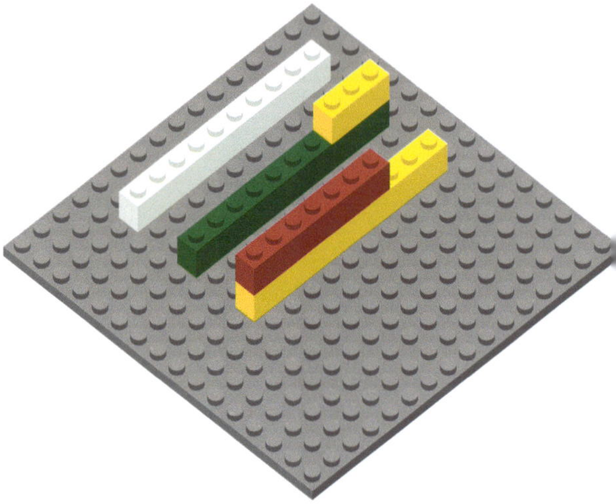

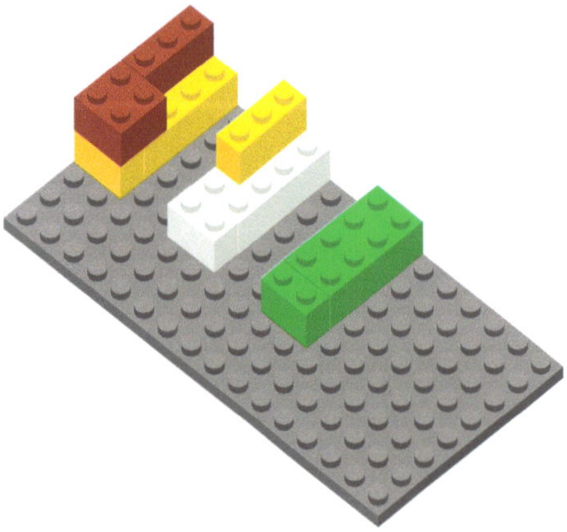

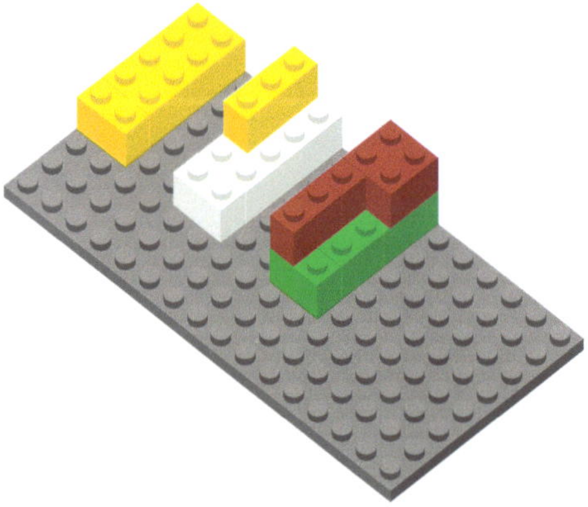

**5.** Have students model all three parts of the problem. Have students draw and label the models and explain the three parts of the problem. Have students write the complete math sentence.

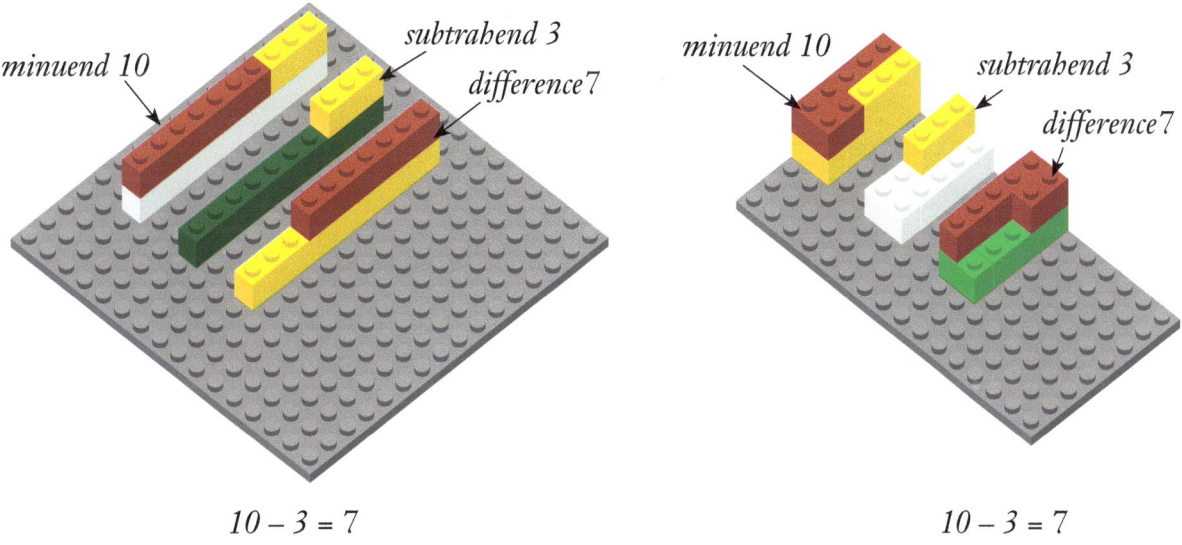

$10 - 3 = 7$  $10 - 3 = 7$

**6.** Build a model for ☐ – 6 = 3. Use 1x10 strips or ten-frames. Ask students to give the math sentence for this model. Have students build the model and draw it.

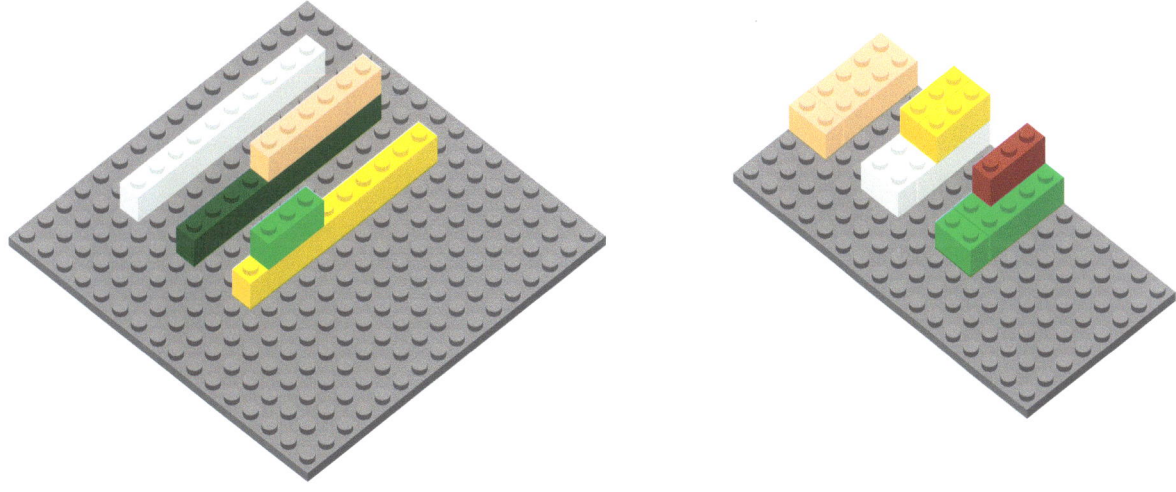

**7.** Point out to students that the start number is missing. Ask students how to find that number. Students should understand the strategy of combining the parts that are known to find the part that is unknown.

DR. SHIRLEY DISSELER | TEACHING SUBTRACTION USING LEGO® BRICKS  **69**

**8.** Move the 6 studs on the center strip to the left strip. Move the 3 studs on the right strip to the left strip. Count the total number of studs now on the left strip. (9)

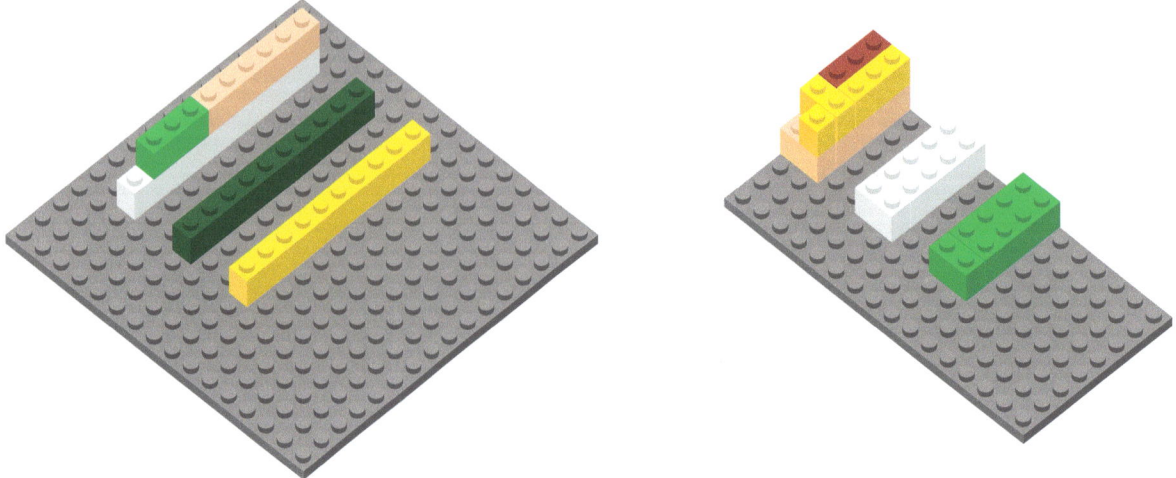

**9.** Work backward on the model to make sure your answer is correct.

**10.** Place bricks on the model to show the *minuend*, *subtrahend*, and *difference*. Have students draw this model, label each part of the problem, and explain how they know the starting number is 9.

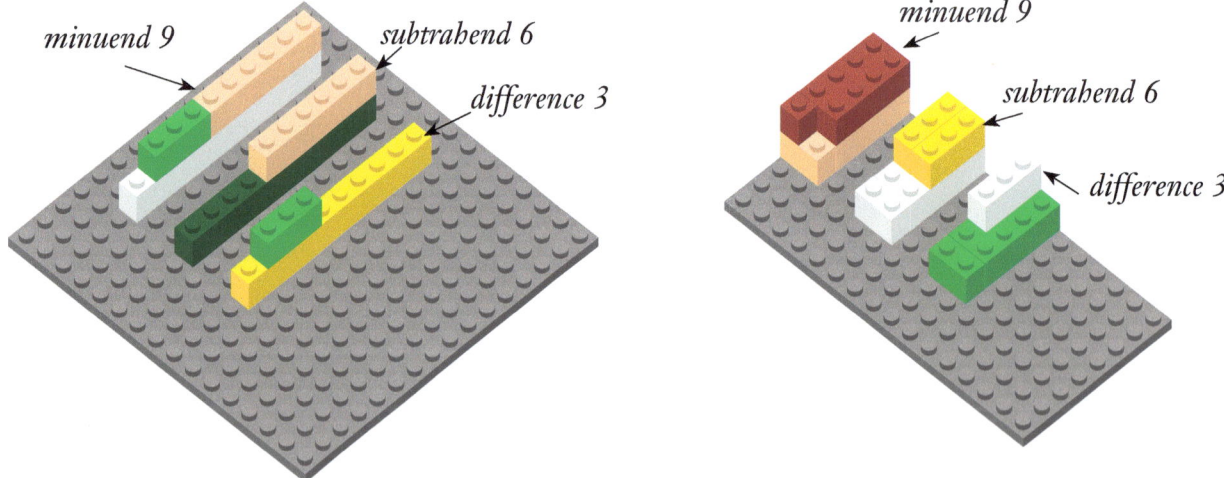

## Part 2: Show What You Know

**1.** Can you build a model that shows this math sentence?

☐ − 4 = 1

You can use a 1x10 strip model or a ten-frame model. Draw your model.

*Note*: 1x10 strip models are shown here, although ten-frame models are equally valid.

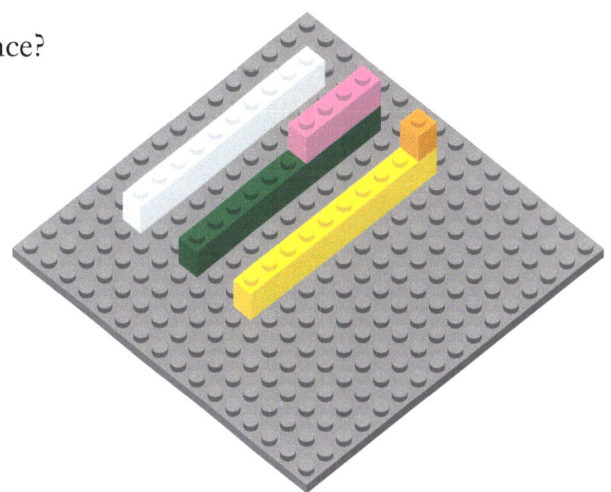

Solve the problem and show all three numbers in the problem on your model. Draw this model and explain how you found the minuend.

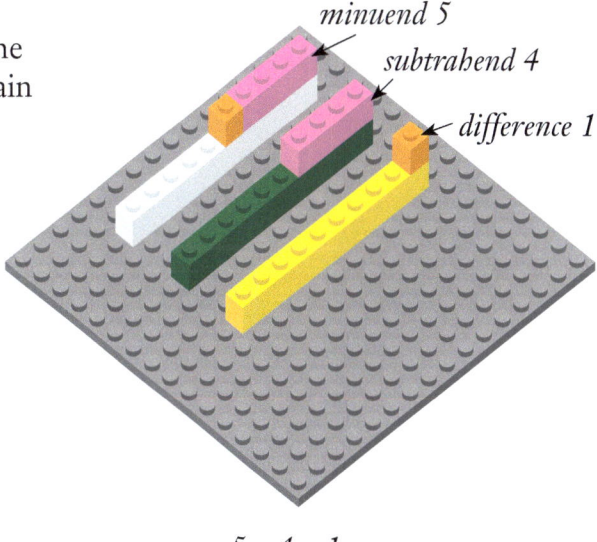

*minuend 5*
*subtrahend 4*
*difference 1*

5 − 4 = 1

**2.** Can you build a model that shows this math sentence?

☐ − 5 = 3

You can use a 1x10 strip model or a ten-frame model. Draw your model.

*Note*: ten-frame models are shown here, although 1x10 strip models are equally valid.

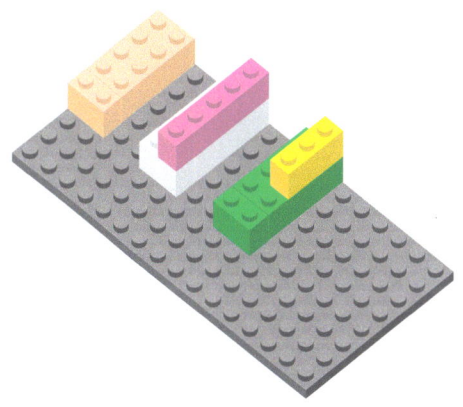

DR. SHIRLEY DISSELER | TEACHING SUBTRACTION USING LEGO® BRICKS  **71**

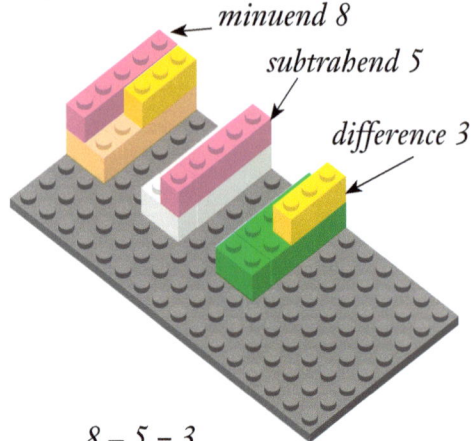

Solve the problem and show all three numbers in the problem on your model. Draw this model and explain how you found the minuend.

$8 - 5 = 3$

**3.** Can you build a model that shows this math sentence?

$\square - 4 = 2$

You can use a 1x10 strip model or a ten-frame model. Draw your model.

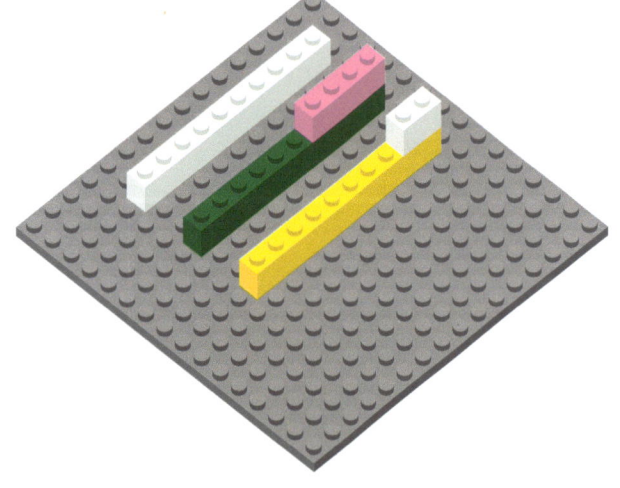

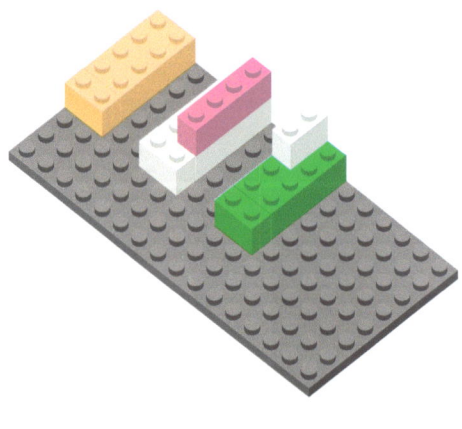

Solve the problem and show all three numbers in the problem on your model. Draw this model and explain how you found the minuend.

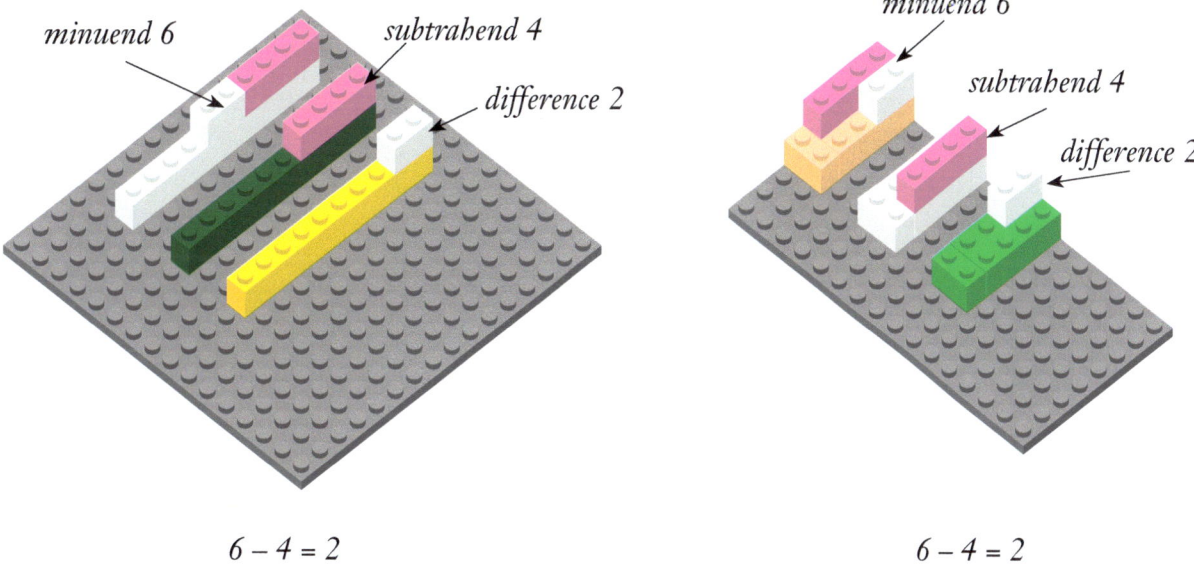

6 – 4 = 2                                     6 – 4 = 2

## Challenge:

Create a problem for a partner to solve. Check to make sure your partner goes through all the steps. Discuss your solutions.

Solutions will vary.

# APPENDIX

- **Suggested Brick Inventory**
- **Student Assessment Chart**
- **Baseplate Paper**

# SUGGESTED BRICK INVENTORY

| SIZE | NUMBER |
|---|---|
| 1x1 | 84 (32 each of two colors and 10 each of two more colors) |
| 1x2 | 25 (10 each of two colors and 5 of a third color) |
| 1x3 | 12 (6 each of two colors) |
| 1x4 | 10 |
| 1x6 | 10 |
| 1x8 | 6 |
| 1x10 | 6 |
| 1x12 | 5 |
| 1x16 | 2 |
| 2x2 | 12 |
| 2x3 | 6 |
| 2x4 | 9 |
| 2x6 | 4 |
| 2x8 | 2 |
| 2x10 | 2 |

# SUBTRACTION
**Student Assessment Chart**

Name _____

| Performance Skill | Not yet | With help | On target | Comments |
|---|---|---|---|---|
| I can model the subtraction of two numbers and label all the parts of a subtraction problem. | | | | |
| I can show and tell what it means to subtract numbers using the correct words. | | | | |
| I can subtract within 20. | | | | |
| I can model how to find the first missing number (start unknown) in a subtraction problem. | | | | |
| I can model how to find the second missing number (change unknown) in a subtraction problem. | | | | |
| I can model how to find the missing result in a subtraction problem. | | | | |
| I can decompose numbers to make sets of tens and ones. | | | | |

# BASEPLATE PAPER

# BASEPLATE PAPER

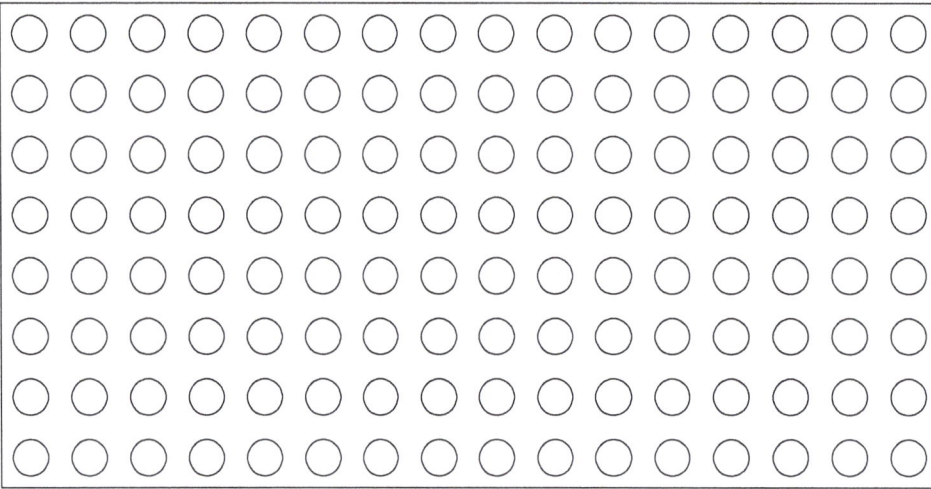

www.ingramcontent.com/pod-product-compliance
Lightning Source LLC
Chambersburg PA
CBHW042013150426
43196CB00002B/34